VUE.JS 3: MASTERING THE FUNDAMENTALS (BUILD MODERN WEB APPS)

Edwin S. Cornish

Table of Contents

Introduction: Welcome to the World of Vue.js 3!

Hey there! So, you're about to embark on a fantastic journey into the world of Vue.js 3. I'm thrilled you've chosen this book as your guide. Whether you're a complete beginner to web development or a seasoned pro looking to add another powerful tool to your belt, Vue.js has something for everyone.

This introduction is designed to set the stage for what you'll learn throughout this book. We'll cover why Vue.js is such a compelling choice for building modern web applications and then get you all set up with the necessary tools for a smooth development experience. Ready? Let's dive in!

• Why Vue.js 3? A Modern Framework for Building Web Apps

In the ever-evolving landscape of web development, choosing the right framework can feel like a daunting task. There are so many options out there! So, why Vue.js 3? Well, here's what makes it stand out:

- **Progressive Adoption:** This is probably Vue.js's biggest strength. You don't have to rewrite your entire application to start using Vue. You can incrementally adopt it, adding it to existing projects piece by piece. Need a fancy interactive element on an existing page? Vue.js can handle that! This flexibility makes it incredibly easy to integrate into projects of any size.
- **Simplicity and Learnability:** Vue.js boasts a gentle learning curve. Its syntax is clean and intuitive, making it relatively easy to pick up, especially if you have a basic understanding of HTML, CSS, and JavaScript. Trust me, you'll be building impressive things in no time!
- **Performance:** Vue.js 3 is fast! The core team put in a *ton* of work to optimize the framework, resulting in significant performance improvements compared to previous versions. This means your applications will be snappier and more responsive, providing a better user experience.
- **Reactivity:** Vue.js's reactivity system is what makes it so dynamic and powerful. It automatically updates the DOM when your data changes, meaning you don't have to manually manipulate the DOM yourself. This makes building interactive UIs a breeze.
- **Composition API:** Vue.js 3 introduced the Composition API, a powerful new way to organize your component logic. It promotes code reusability and makes your components easier to read and maintain. We'll be diving deep into this later in the book!

- **Component-Based Architecture:** Vue.js encourages you to build your applications using reusable components. This not only makes your code more organized but also allows you to build complex UIs more easily.
- **Large and Active Community:** The Vue.js community is incredibly welcoming and supportive. You'll find plenty of resources, tutorials, and libraries to help you along your journey. If you ever get stuck, chances are someone else has already encountered the same problem and found a solution.

Personal Insight: I remember when I first started using Vue.js, I was amazed at how quickly I could build complex interactive elements. Compared to some other frameworks I had used, it felt like a breath of fresh air. The simplicity and elegance of the syntax just clicked with me.

In a Nutshell: Vue.js 3 is a modern, performant, and easy-to-learn framework that's perfect for building a wide range of web applications, from simple interactive elements to complex single-page applications.

• Setting Up Your Development Environment (Node.js, VS Code)

Okay, now that you're excited about Vue.js, let's get your development environment set up. Don't worry, it's not as scary as it sounds! We'll need a few things:

1. **Node.js:** Node.js is a JavaScript runtime environment that allows you to run JavaScript code outside of a web browser. We'll need it for installing and running our development tools.
    - **How to Install:**
        - Go to the official Node.js website: https://nodejs.org/
        - Download the LTS (Long-Term Support) version. This is generally the most stable version.
        - Run the installer and follow the on-screen instructions.
        - **Important:** During the installation, make sure to check the box that says "Automatically install the necessary tools." This will install npm (Node Package Manager), which we'll need in the next step.
    - **Verification:**
        - Open your terminal or command prompt.
        - Type node -v and press Enter. You should see the Node.js version number.

        - Type npm -v and press Enter. You should see the npm version number.
2. **VS Code (Visual Studio Code):** VS Code is a free and powerful code editor that's perfect for Vue.js development.
    - **How to Install:**
        - Go to the official VS Code website: https://code.visualstudio.com/
        - Download the installer for your operating system.
        - Run the installer and follow the on-screen instructions.
    - **Recommended Extensions:** Once you have VS Code installed, I highly recommend installing the following extensions:
        - **Vetur:** Provides syntax highlighting, code completion, and other useful features for Vue.js development. Search for "Vetur" in the VS Code extensions marketplace.
        - **ESLint:** Helps you write clean and consistent JavaScript code. Search for "ESLint" in the VS Code extensions marketplace. You'll likely need to configure it to work with Vue.js, but Vetur can help with that.
        - **Prettier:** Automatically formats your code to make it more readable. Search for "Prettier" in the VS Code extensions marketplace.

Personal Insight: I've tried many code editors over the years, but VS Code has become my go-to. It's lightweight, customizable, and has a fantastic ecosystem of extensions that make development a breeze. I especially love the Vetur extension for Vue.js – it saves me so much time!

That's It!

Congratulations! You've successfully set up your development environment and are ready to start learning Vue.js. In the next chapter, we'll dive into the fundamentals of creating your first Vue.js application. Get ready to build some awesome things!

Key Takeaways:

- Vue.js 3 is a modern, progressive, and performant framework.
- Setting up your development environment is easy with Node.js and VS Code.

- Install the recommended VS Code extensions to enhance your development experience.

This chapter aims to be welcoming and informative, setting the reader up for success in their Vue.js journey. Remember to adjust the tone and level of detail based on your target audience. I hope this draft gives you a great starting point! Let me know if you'd like me to elaborate on any specific sections.

Part 1: Core Concepts

Chapter 1: Your First Vue.js Application – Let's Build Something!

Welcome to your first hands-on experience with Vue.js 3! In this chapter, we're going to build a simple "Hello World" application. This will give you a taste of how Vue.js works and introduce you to some of the core concepts. Don't worry if you don't understand everything perfectly right away – we'll be diving deeper into each concept in the following chapters.

1.1 Creating a Vue Instance – The Heart of Your Application

The Vue instance is truly the engine that drives your Vue.js applications. It's where the magic starts, controlling how your data interacts with the DOM and ultimately shapes the user's experience. Think of it as the central nervous system of your app, receiving and responding to stimuli to create a dynamic and interactive environment. Understanding how to properly create and configure a Vue instance is fundamental to mastering Vue.js.

To get started, let's talk about the createApp function. This is the entry point, the door you walk through to create a Vue instance. The createApp function, imported directly from Vue, accepts a single argument: an options object. This object is where you define all the characteristics of your Vue instance. Let's see this in action:

```
      // main.js

import { createApp } from 'vue';

const app = createApp({
  // Options will go here!
});

app.mount('#app');
```

Notice the import { createApp } from 'vue'; line. This is crucial. Without importing the function, you can't create a Vue app! You then invoke createApp with an options object, saving the result into the app constant. Finally, app.mount('#app'); ties our Vue app to an HTML element. This makes the DOM element with id="app" the *root* of our Vue application.

Everything that Vue controls will happen within this element (or its children).

Understanding the Options Object

Now, let's delve into the heart of the Vue instance: the options object. This is where you configure everything, from the data your application uses to the methods that handle user interactions. Here are some key options to consider:

- **data**: This option is *crucial*. It's a function that returns an object containing the reactive data that will be used in your application. Vue.js tracks any changes to this data, automatically updating the DOM when necessary.

```
const app = createApp({
  data() {
    return {
      message: 'Hello, Vue.js!'
    };
  }
});
```

Here, message becomes a reactive property that we can display in our template.

- **Why a Function?**: You might be wondering why data is a *function* that returns an object, and not just an object directly. This is important! When creating components (which we'll cover later), each component instance needs its own isolated copy of the data. Using a function ensures that each instance gets its own unique data object, preventing accidental data sharing between components.
- **methods**: This option is where you define functions that can be called from your template. These methods are used to handle user events, perform calculations, or update the data in your application.

```
const app = createApp({
  data() {
    return {
      count: 0
    };
  },
  methods: {
    increment() {
      this.count++;
```

```
    }
  }
});
```

Now, you can call the increment method from your template to increase the count property.

- **computed**: Computed properties are functions that calculate a value based on other data in your Vue instance. Vue.js caches the result of a computed property and only re-evaluates it when the dependencies change. This can significantly improve performance, especially for complex calculations.

```
    const app = createApp({
  data() {
    return {
      firstName: 'John',
      lastName: 'Doe'
    };
  },
  computed: {
    fullName() {
      return this.firstName + ' ' + this.lastName;
    }
  }
});
```

The fullName property will automatically update whenever firstName or lastName changes.

- **watch**: Watchers allow you to react to changes in specific data properties. You can use watchers to perform side effects, such as logging data or making API calls.

```
    const app = createApp({
  data() {
    return {
      inputValue: ''
    };
  },
  watch: {
    inputValue(newValue, oldValue) {
      console.log(`inputValue changed from ${oldValue} to
${newValue}`);
      // You could also make an API call here
```

```
      }
    }
});
```

This watcher will log a message to the console every time the inputValue changes.

- **Lifecycle Hooks**: These are special methods that are called at different stages of a Vue instance's lifecycle. They allow you to perform actions at specific times, such as when the component is created, mounted to the DOM, updated, or unmounted. The most common lifecycle hooks are:
  - beforeCreate: Called before the instance is initialized.
  - created: Called after the instance is initialized and data is observed.
  - beforeMount: Called before the instance is mounted to the DOM.
  - mounted: Called after the instance is mounted to the DOM. This is a great place to interact with the DOM.
  - beforeUpdate: Called before the DOM is updated.
  - updated: Called after the DOM is updated.
  - beforeUnmount: Called before the instance is unmounted.
  - unmounted: Called after the instance is unmounted.

Practical Implementation – A Complete Example

Let's put it all together with a complete, working example:

```
      <!DOCTYPE html>
<html>
<head>
  <title>Creating a Vue Instance</title>
  <script
src="https://unpkg.com/vue@3/dist/vue.global.js"></script>
<!-- Using a CDN for simplicity -->
</head>
<body>
  <div id="app">
    <h1>{{ message }}</h1>
    <p>Count: {{ count }}</p>
    <button @click="increment">Increment</button>
    <p>Full Name: {{ fullName }}</p>
    <input type="text" v-model="inputValue" placeholder="Type
something...">
  </div>
```

```
  <script>
    const { createApp } = Vue // Access Vue using the global
object.

    const app = createApp({
      data() {
        return {
          message: 'Hello, Vue.js!',
          count: 0,
          firstName: 'John',
          lastName: 'Doe',
          inputValue: ''
        };
      },
      methods: {
        increment() {
          this.count++;
        }
      },
      computed: {
        fullName() {
          return this.firstName + ' ' + this.lastName;
        }
      },
      watch: {
        inputValue(newValue, oldValue) {
          console.log(`inputValue changed from ${oldValue} to
${newValue}`);
        }
      },
      mounted() {
        console.log('Vue instance mounted!');
      }
    });

    app.mount('#app');
  </script>
</body>
</html>
```

Explanation:

1. **CDN Inclusion:** For simplicity, we're using a CDN to include Vue.js in our HTML. Replace the url to the latest version of Vue.js 3 for the best results. In a real-world project, you'd typically use a build tool like Vue CLI or Vite.

2. **HTML Structure:** We have a div with the ID "app" that serves as the root of our Vue application. We're using interpolation ({{ }}) to display the message, count, and fullName properties. We're also using the v-model directive to bind the inputValue property to an input field.
3. **Vue Instance:** We create a Vue instance with the createApp function. We define the data, methods, computed, and watch options. The mounted lifecycle hook logs a message to the console when the instance is mounted.
4. **Event Handling:** The @click attribute binds the increment method to the button's click event.

Personal Insight: When I first started with Vue.js, I found the options object a little overwhelming. There were so many different options to learn! But once I understood the purpose of each option, it became much easier to structure my Vue applications. Don't be afraid to experiment with the different options and see how they affect your application.

Conclusion:

Creating a Vue instance is the first step in building any Vue.js application. By understanding the createApp function and the options object, you can configure your Vue instance to manage your data, handle user interactions, and create dynamic user interfaces. This foundation is essential for everything else you'll learn in this book. So, take your time, experiment with the code examples, and don't be afraid to ask questions!

This detailed guide provides a comprehensive overview of creating a Vue instance, covering the essential concepts and providing practical code examples. It's designed to be clear, concise, and engaging, making it easy for readers to understand and apply the concepts in their own projects.

1.2 Template Syntax: Data Binding and Expressions – Making Your Data Visible

Now that we've set up our Vue instance, it's time to make our data come alive! Template syntax is how we tell Vue.js to take the data in our Vue instance and display it (or manipulate it) within our HTML. Think of it as the bridge between your JavaScript logic and the visual representation of your application. Mastering template syntax is key to building dynamic and interactive user interfaces.

The primary goal of template syntax is *data binding*. Data binding is the process of connecting data in your Vue instance to elements in your HTML template. When the data changes, the corresponding elements in the template are automatically updated, and vice-versa, in some cases. Vue.js offers several ways to achieve data binding. Let's explore the most important ones.

Interpolation: The Double Curly Braces {{ }}

The simplest and most common form of data binding is *interpolation*. This involves wrapping data properties in double curly braces: {{ }}. Vue.js will then replace the content within the braces with the value of the corresponding data property.

Here's a simple example:

```
<div id="app">
  <h1>{{ message }}</h1>
</div>
```

In this example, Vue.js will look for a property called message in your Vue instance and replace {{ message }} with its value. If message is "Hello, Vue.js!", the rendered HTML will be:

```
<div id="app">
  <h1>Hello, Vue.js!</h1>
</div>
```

Interpolation isn't limited to simple data properties. You can also use JavaScript expressions within the curly braces:

```
<p>{{ firstName + ' ' + lastName }}</p>
<p>{{ count * 2 }}</p>
```

These expressions will be evaluated, and the results will be displayed in the template.

Important Considerations for Expressions:

- **Keep them simple:** While you *can* use JavaScript expressions, it's best to keep them concise and focused on simple data transformations.

- **No statements:** You can't use JavaScript statements (like if statements or loops) within interpolation. For more complex logic, use computed properties or methods (which we'll discuss later).
- **Context:** Inside interpolation, you have access to the properties of your Vue instance.

Directives: Adding Special Powers to Your HTML

Directives are special attributes that begin with the prefix v-. They provide a powerful way to manipulate the DOM based on the data in your Vue instance. Directives essentially add "special powers" to your HTML elements.

Let's explore some of the most important directives:

- **v-bind (Binding Attributes):** The v-bind directive is used to dynamically bind HTML attributes to data in your Vue instance. This is incredibly useful for setting attributes like src, href, class, and style.

```
    <img v-bind:src="imageUrl" alt="My Image">
<a v-bind:href="linkUrl">Click Here</a>
```

  In these examples, the src attribute of the img element is bound to the imageUrl property in your Vue instance, and the href attribute of the a element is bound to the linkUrl property.

  Shorthand: v-bind has a shorthand notation: just use a colon (:).

```
    <img :src="imageUrl" alt="My Image">  <!-- Same as v-
bind:src -->
<a :href="linkUrl">Click Here</a>   <!-- Same as v-bind:href
-->
```

- **v-if (Conditional Rendering):** The v-if directive conditionally renders an element based on a boolean expression. If the expression is true, the element is rendered; otherwise, it is not.

```
    <p v-if="isLoggedIn">Welcome, user!</p>
```

This paragraph will only be displayed if the isLoggedIn property in your Vue instance is true.

- **v-show (Conditional Visibility):** The v-show directive also conditionally renders an element, but it works differently than v-if. Instead of adding or removing the element from the DOM, v-show simply toggles the display CSS property.

```
<p v-show="isVisible">This paragraph is visible!</p>
```

This paragraph will be displayed if the isVisible property is true, and hidden if it is false. The difference is that the paragraph is *always* in the DOM, even when hidden (using display: none;).

Key Difference: v-if vs. v-show: Use v-if when you want to completely remove an element from the DOM if it's not needed. This is more performant if the element is rarely shown or hidden. Use v-show when you need to quickly toggle the visibility of an element, as it avoids the overhead of adding and removing the element from the DOM.

- **v-for (List Rendering):** The v-for directive is used to render a list of items based on an array of data. It iterates over the array and creates a new element for each item.

```
<ul>
  <li v-for="item in items" :key="item.id">{{ item.name
}}</li>
</ul>
```

In this example, items is an array in your Vue instance. For each item in the array, a new li element will be created, and the item.name property will be displayed inside the li element.

The :key Attribute: The :key attribute is *crucial* when using v-for. It provides Vue.js with a unique identifier for each item in the list. This allows Vue.js to efficiently update the DOM when the list changes. Always use a unique and stable key for each item.

- **v-on (Event Handling):** The v-on directive is used to listen for DOM events, such as clicks, mouseovers, and keypresses, and execute a method in your Vue instance when the event occurs.

```
<button v-on:click="handleClick">Click Me</button>
```

  This button will call the handleClick method in your Vue instance when clicked.

  Shorthand: v-on also has a shorthand notation: just use the @ symbol.

```
<button @click="handleClick">Click Me</button>  <!--
Same as v-on:click -->
```

  Event Modifiers: v-on supports *event modifiers*, which are special suffixes that modify the behavior of the event listener. Some common event modifiers include:

  - .stop: Calls event.stopPropagation() to prevent the event from bubbling up the DOM tree.
  - .prevent: Calls event.preventDefault() to prevent the default behavior of the event (e.g., submitting a form).
  - .self: Only triggers the handler if the event was dispatched from the element itself.
  - .once: Ensures the handler is only triggered once.

```
<a @click.prevent="handleClick">Click Me (Prevent
Default)</a>
```

- **v-model (Two-Way Data Binding):** The v-model directive creates a *two-way data binding* between an input element and a data property in your Vue instance. This means that when the user types something into the input field, the data property is automatically updated, and vice-versa.

```
<input type="text" v-model="message">
<p>You typed: {{ message }}</p>
```

As the user types into the input field, the message property will be updated in real time, and the paragraph below will display the current value of message. v-model simplifies handling user input significantly.

Practical Implementation – A Complete Example

Let's combine these concepts into a complete example:

```
    <!DOCTYPE html>
<html>
<head>
  <title>Template Syntax and Data Binding</title>
  <script
src="https://unpkg.com/vue@3/dist/vue.global.js"></script>
</head>
<body>
  <div id="app">
    <h1>{{ title }}</h1>
    <p v-if="isLoggedIn">Welcome, {{ username }}!</p>
    <p v-else>Please log in.</p>

    <ul>
      <li v-for="item in items" :key="item.id">{{ item.name
}} - Price: ${{ item.price }}</li>
    </ul>

    <button @click="toggleLogin">Toggle Login</button>

    <input type="text" v-model="newTodo" placeholder="Add a
todo...">
    <button @click="addTodo">Add</button>

    <ul>
      <li v-for="todo in todos" :key="todo.id">{{ todo.text
}}</li>
    </ul>
  </div>

  <script>
    const { createApp } = Vue;

    const app = createApp({
      data() {
        return {
          title: 'My Awesome App',
          isLoggedIn: false,
          username: 'JohnDoe',
          items: [
```

```
          { id: 1, name: 'Apple', price: 1.00 },
          { id: 2, name: 'Banana', price: 0.50 },
          { id: 3, name: 'Orange', price: 0.75 }
        ],
        newTodo: '',
        todos: []
      };
    },
    methods: {
      toggleLogin() {
        this.isLoggedIn = !this.isLoggedIn;
      },
      addTodo() {
        if (this.newTodo.trim() !== '') {
          this.todos.push({
            id: Date.now(),  // Simple unique ID
            text: this.newTodo
          });
          this.newTodo = ''; // Clear the input
        }
      }
    }
  });

  app.mount('#app');
 </script>
</body>
</html>
```

Explanation:

1. **Data:** We have various data properties like title, isLoggedIn, items, newTodo, and todos.
2. **Conditional Rendering:** We use v-if and v-else to display different messages based on the isLoggedIn property.
3. **List Rendering:** We use v-for to display a list of items from the items array.
4. **Event Handling:** We use @click to call the toggleLogin and addTodo methods when the buttons are clicked.
5. **Two-Way Data Binding:** We use v-model to bind the newTodo property to the input field.

Personal Insight: I remember the first time I used v-model. It felt like magic! It was so much easier than manually handling input events and updating the data. It's one of the features that makes Vue.js so enjoyable to work with.

Conclusion:

Mastering template syntax and data binding is fundamental to building dynamic Vue.js applications. By understanding interpolation and directives, you can connect your data to the DOM, manipulate HTML elements, and create interactive user interfaces. Practice these concepts, experiment with the code examples, and you'll be well on your way to building amazing Vue.js applications. The next step is exploring components, which will allow you to build reusable UI elements. Get ready for the next level!

1.3 Directives: Manipulating the DOM – Taking Control

We've already touched on directives briefly, but now let's really dive in and explore how they allow us to manipulate the Document Object Model (DOM) in powerful and efficient ways within our Vue.js applications. Think of directives as special attributes that give our HTML elements superpowers. They let us hook into the Vue.js reactivity system and dynamically control the behavior and appearance of our elements.

Remember, directives are special HTML attributes that start with the v- prefix. Vue.js provides a set of built-in directives, and we can even create our own custom directives (we'll explore that later). However, let's focus on the core directives that you'll use most often.

Revisiting the Essentials (and Adding Depth):

Let's build on what we've already learned and add some crucial details:

- **v-if, v-else-if, and v-else (Conditional Rendering - Revisited):** These directives provide powerful conditional rendering capabilities. v-if renders an element based on the truthiness of an expression. v-else-if provides an alternative condition, and v-else renders if all previous conditions are false.

```
    <div v-if="type === 'A'">
  Type A
</div>
<div v-else-if="type === 'B'">
  Type B
</div>
<div v-else>
  Unknown Type
</div>
```

Important Performance Note: As we mentioned before, v-if adds or removes the element from the DOM, which can be more performant if the condition rarely changes. However, excessive use of v-if can lead to layout thrashing if elements are frequently added and removed.

- **v-show (Conditional Visibility - Revisited):** As we know, v-show toggles the display CSS property to show or hide an element. The key difference is that the element *always* remains in the DOM.

  When to Choose v-if vs. v-show: Use v-if for conditions that rarely change or when you want to completely remove an element from the DOM. Use v-show when you need to quickly toggle visibility without the overhead of adding and removing elements.

- **v-for (List Rendering - Revisited):** v-for iterates over an array or object and renders an element for each item. We've seen the basics, but let's add some more advanced usage.

```
<ul>
  <li v-for="(item, index) in items" :key="item.id">
    {{ index + 1 }}. {{ item.name }}
  </li>
</ul>
```

In this example, we're accessing both the item and the index within the loop. The index represents the current position of the item in the array (starting from 0).

Iterating over Objects: You can also use v-for to iterate over the properties of an object:

```
<ul>
  <li v-for="(value, key, index) in myObject" :key="key">
    {{ index + 1 }}. {{ key }}: {{ value }}
  </li>
</ul>
```

In this case, value represents the value of the property, key represents the property name, and index represents the position of the property in the object. Note that the order of properties in an object is not guaranteed to be consistent across browsers.

The key Attribute - Emphasized Again!: *Never forget the :key attribute when using v-for!* It's crucial for Vue.js to efficiently track changes in the list and update the DOM correctly. Use a unique and stable identifier for each item. If you don't have a natural unique ID, you can use the index, but be aware that this can lead to performance issues if the list is frequently reordered.

- **v-bind (Binding Attributes - Revisited):** We've seen how to bind simple attributes. Now, let's explore dynamic classes and styles.

  Dynamic Classes: You can dynamically add or remove CSS classes using v-bind:class. You can pass an object, an array, or a string.

  - **Object Syntax:**

```
<div :class="{ active: isActive, 'text-bold': isBold
}">
  This element can be active and/or bold.
</div>
```

    The active class will be added if isActive is true, and the text-bold class will be added if isBold is true.

  - **Array Syntax:**

```
<div :class="[activeClass, errorClass]">
  This element will have the classes defined in activeClass
and errorClass.
</div>
```

    activeClass and errorClass should be strings containing the class names.

  Dynamic Styles: You can dynamically set inline styles using v-bind:style. You can pass an object or an array of objects.

  - **Object Syntax:**

```
<div :style="{ color: textColor, fontSize: fontSize +
'px' }">
  This element's style is dynamically set.
</div>
```

textColor and fontSize should be data properties in your Vue instance.

- **Array Syntax (Rarely Used):** You can pass an array of style objects, but this is less common.

- **v-on (Event Handling - Revisited):** We've seen the basics of event handling. Now, let's explore more event modifiers and keyboard events.

  Common Event Modifiers (Recap and Expansion):

  - .stop: event.stopPropagation() - Prevents the event from bubbling up.
  - .prevent: event.preventDefault() - Prevents the default event behavior.
  - .self: Only triggers the handler if the event originated from the element itself.
  - .capture: Uses the capture mode when adding the event listener.
  - .once: The event handler will be invoked at most once.
  - .passive: Indicates that the event listener will not call preventDefault(). This can improve scrolling performance.

  Keyboard Event Modifiers: Vue.js provides convenient modifiers for listening to specific keyboard events:

```
<input @keyup.enter="submitForm">  <!-- Only triggers
on Enter key -->
<input @keyup.esc="cancel">      <!-- Only triggers on Escape
key -->
```

You can also use system modifier keys (Ctrl, Alt, Shift, Meta):

```
<input @keyup.ctrl.enter="save"> <!-- Triggers only on
Ctrl+Enter -->
```

Using the $event Object: You can access the native DOM event object using $event in your template.

```
<button @click="handleClick($event)">Click Me</button>

methods: {
  handleClick(event) {
    console.log(event.target); // Access the button element
  }
}
```

- **v-model (Two-Way Data Binding - Revisited):** While we covered the basics, v-model also has modifiers for more precise control:
    - .lazy: Updates the data only after a "change" event (e.g., when the input loses focus).
    - .number: Automatically converts the input value to a number.
    - .trim: Automatically trims whitespace from the input value.

```
<input type="text" v-model.trim="message">  <!-- Trims
whitespace -->
<input type="number" v-model.number="age"> <!-- Converts to
number -->
```

A More Comprehensive Example:

Let's put these directives to work in a slightly more complex example:

```
<!DOCTYPE html>
<html>
<head>
  <title>Directives in Action</title>
  <script
src="https://unpkg.com/vue@3/dist/vue.global.js"></script>
  <style>
    .active {
      background-color: lightblue;
    }
    .error {
      color: red;
    }
  </style>
</head>
<body>
  <div id="app">
    <h1 :class="{error: hasError}">{{ title }}</h1>
```

```
    <div v-if="showDetails">
      <h2>Details:</h2>
      <p>Username: {{ username }}</p>
      <p>Email: {{ email }}</p>
    </div>
    <button @click="showDetails = !showDetails">Toggle
Details</button>

    <ul>
      <li v-for="(item, index) in items" :key="item.id"
:class="{ active: selectedIndex === index }">
        {{ index + 1 }}. {{ item.name }} - Price: ${{
item.price }}
        <button @click="selectedIndex =
index">Select</button>
      </li>
    </ul>

    <input type="text" v-model.trim="newTodo"
@keyup.enter="addTodo" placeholder="Add a todo...">
    <ul>
      <li v-for="todo in todos" :key="todo.id">{{ todo.text
}}</li>
    </ul>
  </div>

  <script>
    const { createApp } = Vue;

    const app = createApp({
      data() {
        return {
          title: 'Directive Demo',
          hasError: false,
          showDetails: false,
          username: 'ExampleUser',
          email: 'example@example.com',
          items: [
            { id: 1, name: 'Laptop', price: 1200 },
            { id: 2, name: 'Mouse', price: 25 },
            { id: 3, name: 'Keyboard', price: 75 }
          ],
          newTodo: '',
          todos: [],
          selectedIndex: null
        };
      },
      methods: {
        addTodo() {
          if (this.newTodo.trim() !== '') {
```

```
            this.todos.push({ id: Date.now(), text:
this.newTodo });
            this.newTodo = '';
          }
        }
      }
    });

    app.mount('#app');
  </script>
</body>
</html>
```

Key improvements in this example:

- **Dynamic Classes:** The h1 element has a dynamic class that changes its color based on the hasError property.
- **Toggling Visibility:** The "Details" section is shown or hidden using v-if and a toggle button.
- **Selected Item:** The list items have a class that changes their background color based on the selectedIndex property.
- **Keyboard Event Handling:** The addTodo method is called when the Enter key is pressed in the input field.

Personal Insight: Directives were one of the first things that really "clicked" for me when learning Vue.js. They felt like a natural extension of HTML, and they made it so much easier to build dynamic and interactive user interfaces. Experimenting with the different directives and their modifiers is a great way to deepen your understanding of Vue.js.

Conclusion:

Directives are essential tools for manipulating the DOM in Vue.js applications. By mastering the core directives like v-if, v-show, v-for, v-bind, v-on, and v-model, you can create dynamic and interactive user interfaces with ease. Remember to practice with the code examples and explore the different modifiers to unleash the full power of directives. In the next section, we will explore Components, which will give you the ultimate power to build large scale applications

1.4 Hello World: Options API vs. Composition API – A Sneak Peek

Now that you've got a basic grasp of Vue.js fundamentals, it's time to introduce you to a pivotal shift in how you structure your Vue components: the Composition API. This is a *sneak peek*, remember – we'll be diving much deeper into the Composition API in later chapters. But it's important to get a taste of it early on, to understand the evolution of Vue.js and the benefits it offers.

For years, the primary way to organize Vue components was the **Options API**. It's what you've been using in the previous sections. However, Vue.js 3 introduced the **Composition API**, a fundamentally different approach that offers improved code organization, reusability, and TypeScript support.

Think of it like this: the Options API provides a predefined structure for your components, like a template. The Composition API gives you more freedom to organize your code as you see fit, like building with Lego blocks. Both approaches have their strengths and weaknesses, and understanding both is crucial for becoming a well-rounded Vue.js developer.

The Options API: Structured and Familiar

The Options API organizes component logic into predefined options: data, methods, computed, watch, and lifecycle hooks. This structure is easy to learn and provides a clear separation of concerns.

Let's revisit our "Hello World" example using the Options API:

```
    <!DOCTYPE html>
<html>
<head>
  <title>Options API Hello World</title>
  <script
src="https://unpkg.com/vue@3/dist/vue.global.js"></script>
</head>
<body>
  <div id="app">
    <h1>{{ message }}</h1>
  </div>

  <script>
    const { createApp } = Vue;
```

```
    const app = createApp({
      data() {
        return {
          message: 'Hello from Options API!'
        };
      }
    });

    app.mount('#app');
  </script>
</body>
</html>
```

Key characteristics of the Options API:

- **Organization:** Code is organized into distinct options (data, methods, etc.).
- **this Context:** Inside the options, you access component properties using this.
- **Simplicity:** Easy to learn and get started with, especially for smaller components.
- **Limited Reusability:** Sharing logic between components can be challenging.

The Composition API: Flexible and Reusable

The Composition API, on the other hand, allows you to organize component logic using functions. You define reactive state using ref and reactive, and you expose these properties to the template by returning them from the setup() function.

Here's the same "Hello World" example using the Composition API:

```
    <!DOCTYPE html>
<html>
<head>
  <title>Composition API Hello World</title>
  <script
src="https://unpkg.com/vue@3/dist/vue.global.js"></script>
</head>
<body>
  <div id="app">
    <h1>{{ message }}</h1>
  </div>
```

```
  <script>
    const { createApp, ref } = Vue;

    const app = createApp({
      setup() {
        const message = ref('Hello from Composition API!');

        return {
          message
        };
      }
    });

    app.mount('#app');
  </script>
</body>
</html>
```

Key characteristics of the Composition API:

- **setup() Function:** All component logic is defined within the setup() function.
- **Reactivity with ref and reactive:** You create reactive data using ref for single values and reactive for objects.
- **Explicit Exposure:** You explicitly expose the properties you want to use in the template by returning them from setup().
- **Improved Reusability:** You can easily extract and reuse logic across multiple components by creating composable functions.
- **Better TypeScript Support:** The Composition API is more type-friendly, making it easier to use with TypeScript.

Dissecting the Composition API Example:

1. **import { createApp, ref } from Vue;**: We now import the ref function along with createApp. ref is essential for creating reactive variables in the Composition API.
2. **setup() { ... }**: The setup function is the heart of the Composition API. It's where you define your component's reactive state, computed properties, methods, and lifecycle hooks. It's executed *before* the component is created.
3. **const message = ref('Hello from Composition API!');**: This creates a reactive variable named message using the ref function. ref takes an initial value as its argument. Think of ref as creating a "reactive

container" that holds a value. To access the value inside a ref, you use the .value property (though this isn't needed in the template).

4. **return { message };**: This *explicitly* exposes the message variable to the component's template. Only properties returned from the setup function are available in the template.

Why the Composition API? (A Glimpse)

The Composition API might seem more complex at first, but it solves some important problems:

- **Improved Code Organization:** As components grow larger, the Options API can become difficult to manage. Related logic can be scattered across different options. The Composition API allows you to group related logic together in functions, making your code more readable and maintainable.
- **Enhanced Reusability:** The Composition API makes it easy to extract and reuse logic across multiple components. You can create composable functions that encapsulate specific pieces of functionality and then import and use those functions in any component that needs them.
- **Better TypeScript Support:** The Composition API is more type-friendly than the Options API, making it easier to use with TypeScript and catch type errors early on.

Which API to Use (For Now)?

In this book, we'll start by focusing on the Options API. It's a great way to learn the fundamentals of Vue.js and provides a solid foundation for understanding more advanced concepts. Later in the book, we'll transition to the Composition API and explore its benefits in more detail.

Personal Insight: When I first encountered the Composition API, I was a bit skeptical. I was comfortable with the Options API, and the Composition API seemed more verbose. However, as I started building larger and more complex components, I realized the power and flexibility of the Composition API. It's now my preferred way to organize Vue components.

Conclusion:

This "Sneak Peek" has introduced you to the two main approaches to building Vue.js components: the Options API and the Composition API. The

Options API provides a structured and familiar approach, while the Composition API offers more flexibility and reusability. We'll be exploring both of these APIs in more detail throughout the book. For now, focus on understanding the Options API, and get ready to dive deeper into the world of Vue.js! In the next chapter, we will start exploring components.

Chapter 2: Mastering Template Syntax – Bringing Your Data to Life

Welcome back! In Chapter 1, we got our feet wet with some basic template syntax. Now, it's time to really dive deep and become masters of manipulating the DOM with Vue's powerful template features. This chapter is all about unlocking the full potential of your Vue.js applications by creating dynamic and interactive user interfaces. So, buckle up, and let's get started!

2.1 Interpolation and Data Binding: Beyond the Basics – Connecting Data to Your Templates

In the world of Vue.js, template syntax is the language we use to tell the framework how to render our data within the DOM. Among the various tools in our template arsenal, interpolation and data binding stand out as fundamental techniques for creating dynamic and responsive user interfaces. They form the bedrock of how we connect our data, residing within the Vue instance, to the visual representation of our application.

While we touched on these concepts in the introductory chapter, it's crucial to delve deeper and understand their nuances and limitations. This section is dedicated to truly mastering these essential techniques.

Interpolation: Displaying Data with Elegance and Simplicity

Interpolation, achieved using the double curly braces {{ }}, is the most direct and intuitive way to display data in your templates. It allows you to embed data properties and JavaScript expressions directly within your HTML.

```
    <div id="app">
  <h1>{{ message }}</h1>
  <p>The current count is: {{ count }}</p>
</div>
```

In this simple example, the {{ message }} and {{ count }} placeholders will be dynamically replaced with the corresponding values from your Vue instance's data option. If message holds the value "Hello, Vue.js!" and count is set to 5, the resulting HTML would be:

```
<div id="app">
  <h1>Hello, Vue.js!</h1>
  <p>The current count is: 5</p>
</div>
```

This mechanism works by Vue scanning the template and creating a "watcher" for each expression inside the curly braces. Any changes to the data properties that these expressions depend on trigger an update in the DOM.

Beyond Simple Values: Exploring the Power of Expressions

Interpolation isn't limited to displaying simple data properties. You can also use JavaScript expressions within the curly braces to perform calculations, format data, or even call functions.

Consider these examples:

```
<p>Full Name: {{ firstName + ' ' + lastName }}</p>
<p>Double the Count: {{ count * 2 }}</p>
<p>Is Logged In: {{ isLoggedIn ? 'Yes' : 'No' }}</p>
<p>Formatted Date: {{ formatDate(date) }}</p>
```

Here, we are performing string concatenation, arithmetic operations, using a ternary operator for conditional display, and calling a method to format a date. While this showcases the flexibility of interpolation, it also highlights its limitations.

The Caveats: Mind the Complexity

While interpolation allows for expressions, it's essential to remember that these expressions should be kept simple and focused on data transformation rather than complex logic. Interpolation isn't the place for complex calculations, conditional statements, or variable declarations. Avoid attempting anything more complex than a basic one-liner within the curly braces.

Why the Limitation?

Complex expressions within interpolation can lead to performance issues and reduced code readability. Every time the component re-renders, these expressions are re-evaluated. If an expression involves expensive calculations or API calls, it can significantly impact the application's performance.

Moreover, burying complex logic within the template makes it harder to understand, test, and maintain the component. When you or another developer looks at the component in the future, they'll have to unravel the logic embedded in the template, which can be time-consuming and error-prone.

A Better Approach: Computed Properties and Methods

For complex logic or data transformations, computed properties and methods are the preferred alternatives. They offer improved performance, readability, and testability.

Computed properties allow you to define properties that are derived from other data properties. Vue.js automatically caches the results of computed properties, so they are only re-evaluated when their dependencies change.

Methods allow you to define functions that can be called from your template. While you can call methods directly within interpolation, it's generally recommended to use computed properties for data transformations and methods for handling events and actions.

Data Binding with v-bind: Dynamically Controlling Attributes

While interpolation excels at displaying text content, it falls short when it comes to dynamically controlling HTML attributes. This is where v-bind comes to the rescue. v-bind, also known as attribute binding, allows you to dynamically bind HTML attributes to data properties in your Vue instance.

Syntax and Usage

The basic syntax for v-bind is as follows:

```
<element v-bind:attribute="dataProperty"></element>
```

Here, element represents the HTML element whose attribute you want to bind, attribute is the HTML attribute you want to control, and dataProperty is the data property in your Vue instance that will determine the attribute's value.

Vue offers shorthand for v-bind, using a simple colon : before the attribute name.

```
<element :attribute="dataProperty"></element>
```

Examples

Let's look at some examples to illustrate how v-bind works.

- **Binding the src attribute of an <img> element:**

  ```
  <img :src="imageUrl" alt="My Image">
  ```

  Here, the src attribute of the <img> element is bound to the imageUrl data property in your Vue instance. As the value of imageUrl changes, the src attribute will be automatically updated, causing the image to change.

- **Binding the href attribute of an <a> element:**

  ```
  <a :href="linkUrl">Click Here</a>
  ```

  Similarly, the href attribute of the <a> element is bound to the linkUrl property, allowing the link's destination to be dynamically set.

- **Binding the class attribute to add or remove CSS classes dynamically:**

```
    <div :class="{ active: isActive, 'text-bold': isBold
}">
  This element has dynamic classes.
</div>
```

  This powerful technique allows you to add or remove CSS classes based on the values of isActive and isBold properties. The active class will be applied only when isActive is true, and the text-bold class will be applied only when isBold is true.

- **Binding inline styles:**

```
    <div :style="{ color: textColor, fontSize: fontSize + 'px' }">
      This element has dynamic styles.
    </div>
```

With this you can dynamically style your components.

Personal Insight: The Power of Dynamic Classes

Early in my Vue.js journey, I was blown away by the power of dynamic class binding. It made it incredibly easy to create responsive and interactive user interfaces that adapted to different states and user actions. I was able to create components that seamlessly transitioned between different visual styles, providing a smooth and engaging user experience.

Important Note: The style Attribute

When using v-bind:style (or its shorthand, :style), remember that style properties should be written in camelCase (e.g., fontSize, backgroundColor) rather than kebab-case (e.g., font-size, background-color). Vue.js automatically handles the conversion to kebab-case when applying the styles to the element.

Putting it All Together: A Practical Example

Let's integrate these concepts into a practical example:

```
<!DOCTYPE html>
<html>
<head>
  <title>Interpolation and Data Binding</title>
  <script src="https://unpkg.com/vue@3/dist/vue.global.js"></script>
</head>
<body>
  <div id="app">
    <h1>{{ title }}</h1>
    <img :src="imageUrl" :alt="imageAltText">
    <p>Price: ${{ price }}</p>
    <p :class="{ 'discounted': onSale }">
      {{ onSale ? 'On Sale!' : 'Regular Price' }}
    </p>
  </div>

  <script>
```

```
    const { createApp } = Vue;

    const app = createApp({
      data() {
        return {
          title: 'Product Details',
          imageUrl: 'https://via.placeholder.com/150',
          imageAltText: 'A placeholder image',
          price: 25.99,
          onSale: true
        };
      }
    });

    app.mount('#app');
  </script>
</body>
</html>
```

In this example, we are using interpolation to display the title and price properties. We are using v-bind to dynamically set the src and alt attributes of the <img> element. We are also using v-bind:class to apply the discounted class to the <p> element if the onSale property is true.

Personal Insight: The Aha! Moment

I recall a moment when the concepts of interpolation and data binding truly clicked for me. I was building a dynamic form where the labels and input fields needed to change based on user selections. By combining interpolation and v-bind, I was able to create a truly dynamic and interactive form with minimal code. It was then that I realized the true power and elegance of Vue's template syntax.

Conclusion: Mastering the Fundamentals

Interpolation and data binding are the cornerstones of Vue.js template syntax. They provide the foundation for connecting your data to the DOM and creating dynamic and interactive user interfaces.

Remember that while interpolation offers a simple way to display data, it's essential to limit the complexity of expressions within the curly braces. For more complex logic, computed properties and methods are the preferred alternatives.

v-bind, on the other hand, unlocks the power of dynamically controlling HTML attributes, allowing you to create truly responsive and adaptable applications.

By mastering these fundamental techniques, you'll be well-equipped to tackle more advanced concepts and build stunning Vue.js applications.

2.2 Conditional Rendering (v-if, v-show): Controlling Visibility – Showing and Hiding Elements with Precision

Conditional rendering is a crucial aspect of building dynamic and interactive web applications. It's the art of selectively displaying or hiding elements based on certain conditions, making your user interfaces more responsive and adaptable. Vue.js provides two powerful directives for achieving conditional rendering: v-if and v-show. While both serve the purpose of controlling visibility, they operate in fundamentally different ways, and understanding their nuances is essential for building performant and maintainable Vue.js applications.

Think of conditional rendering as giving your HTML elements the power of choice. They can decide whether or not to reveal themselves based on the current state of your application. This allows you to create interfaces that adapt to user actions, data changes, and various other scenarios.

v-if: The Decisive Director – Adding and Removing Elements

The v-if directive is the most straightforward way to conditionally render elements in Vue.js. It adds or removes elements from the DOM entirely based on the truthiness of the expression it evaluates. If the expression is true, the element is rendered; if it's false, the element is completely removed from the DOM.

```
    <div id="app">
  <p v-if="isLoggedIn">Welcome, user!</p>
  <p v-else>Please log in.</p>
</div>
```

In this example, the "Welcome, user!" paragraph will only be rendered if the isLoggedIn data property in your Vue instance is true. If isLoggedIn is false, the paragraph will be completely removed from the DOM, as if it never existed. Similarly, the "Please log in." paragraph will be rendered only when isLoggedIn is false due to the v-else directive.

Using v-else-if for Multiple Conditions

You can chain multiple conditions together using v-else-if, creating more complex conditional rendering scenarios.

```
      <div v-if="type === 'A'">
  Type A content
</div>
<div v-else-if="type === 'B'">
  Type B content
</div>
<div v-else>
  Default content
</div>
```

Here, the content displayed depends on the value of the type property. If type is "A", the "Type A content" div will be rendered. If type is "B", the "Type B content" div will be rendered. If type is anything else, the "Default content" div will be rendered.

The <template> Element and v-if

Sometimes, you might want to conditionally render multiple elements without adding a wrapper element to your DOM structure. This is where the <template> element comes in handy. You can use <template> with v-if to conditionally render a block of elements without creating an extra DOM node.

```
      <template v-if="isLoggedIn">
  <h1>Welcome!</h1>
  <p>You are logged in.</p>
</template>
```

The <template> element itself is not rendered in the DOM. Only its children are rendered, and only if the isLoggedIn condition is true. This allows you to group related elements and conditionally render them as a single unit.

v-show: The Master of Disguise – Toggling Visibility with CSS

The v-show directive provides an alternative approach to conditional rendering. Instead of adding or removing elements from the DOM, v-show simply toggles the display CSS property of the element. If the expression is true, the element's display property is set to its default value (usually block or inline). If the expression is false, the element's display property is set to none, effectively hiding the element.

```
    <div id="app">
  <p v-show="isVisible">This paragraph is visible!</p>
</div>
```

In this example, the "This paragraph is visible!" paragraph will be displayed if the isVisible data property is true, and hidden if it's false. However, unlike v-if, the paragraph element *always* remains in the DOM, even when it's hidden. It's merely hidden from view using CSS.

v-if vs. v-show: The Key Differences – Choosing the Right Tool

The crucial difference between v-if and v-show lies in how they manipulate the DOM. v-if adds or removes elements entirely, while v-show simply toggles their visibility using CSS. This difference has significant implications for performance and application behavior.

- **Performance:**
    - v-if: Has higher "toggle cost" because it involves adding and removing elements from the DOM, which can be computationally expensive, especially for complex elements with many children. However, it has lower "initial render cost" because it doesn't render the element at all if the condition is initially false.
    - v-show: Has lower "toggle cost" because it only involves toggling the display property, which is a relatively cheap operation. However, it has higher "initial render cost" because it renders the element regardless of the initial condition.
- **Compilation:**
    - v-if: Elements are not compiled if the condition is initially false.

- v-show: Elements are always compiled, regardless of the condition.

- **Use Cases:**
    - v-if: Use v-if when the condition is unlikely to change frequently, or when you want to completely prevent an element from being rendered if it's not needed. This is ideal for elements that are displayed only under specific circumstances, such as user login status or feature flags.
    - v-show: Use v-show when the condition is likely to change frequently, and you need to quickly toggle the visibility of an element. This is ideal for elements that are shown and hidden frequently based on user interactions, such as tooltips, menus, or loading indicators.

Personal Insight: The Performance Pitfalls

Early on in my Vue.js development, I didn't fully grasp the performance implications of v-if and v-show. I used v-if indiscriminately, even for elements that were frequently toggled. This resulted in noticeable performance issues, especially on older devices. Once I understood the difference between the two directives, I was able to optimize my code and improve the application's responsiveness significantly.

Practical Example: Combining v-if and v-show

Let's create a practical example that demonstrates the use of both v-if and v-show:

```
    <!DOCTYPE html>
<html>
<head>
  <title>Conditional Rendering</title>
  <script
src="https://unpkg.com/vue@3/dist/vue.global.js"></script>
</head>
<body>
  <div id="app">
    <button @click="isLoggedIn = !isLoggedIn">
      {{ isLoggedIn ? 'Log Out' : 'Log In' }}
    </button>

    <div v-if="isLoggedIn">
      <h1>Welcome, user!</h1>
      <p>You are now logged in.</p>
    </div>
```

```
    <div v-show="isLoading">
      <p>Loading...</p>
    </div>
  </div>

  <script>
    const { createApp } = Vue;

    const app = createApp({
      data() {
        return {
          isLoggedIn: false,
          isLoading: false
        };
      },
      mounted() {
        // Simulate loading data
        this.isLoading = true;
        setTimeout(() => {
          this.isLoading = false;
        }, 2000);
      }
    });

    app.mount('#app');
  </script>
</body>
</html>
```

In this example, we use v-if to conditionally render the welcome message based on the isLoggedIn property. The welcome message is only displayed when the user is logged in.

We use v-show to display a loading indicator while the data is being loaded. The loading indicator is shown for 2 seconds using a setTimeout function in the mounted lifecycle hook.

Personal Insight: The Power of a Loading Indicator

Adding a simple loading indicator can significantly improve the user experience. It provides visual feedback to the user, letting them know that something is happening in the background. Without a loading indicator, the user might think that the application is frozen or broken.

Conclusion: Mastering Conditional Rendering

Conditional rendering is an essential skill for any Vue.js developer. By understanding the nuances of v-if and v-show, you can create dynamic and responsive user interfaces that adapt to different states and user interactions.

Remember that v-if adds or removes elements from the DOM, making it ideal for conditions that rarely change. v-show, on the other hand, toggles visibility using CSS, making it ideal for frequent visibility changes.

By carefully choosing the right directive for each scenario, you can optimize the performance and maintainability of your Vue.js applications. In the next section, we will explore components, a powerful way to break down your application into reusable building blocks.

2.3 List Rendering (v-for): Mastering Iteration – Displaying Data Collections with Ease

In the realm of web development, we often deal with collections of data: lists of products, users, articles, or any other type of information. Displaying these collections efficiently and dynamically is a fundamental task. Vue.js provides the v-for directive, a powerful tool that simplifies the process of iterating over arrays and objects, rendering elements for each item in the collection. Mastering v-for is essential for building dynamic and data-driven user interfaces.

Think of v-for as your personal army of DOM element creators. Give it a list and a template, and it will diligently generate the corresponding HTML elements, connecting them to the data in your collection. This not only saves you from writing repetitive code but also ensures that your interface stays in sync with your data, automatically updating whenever the collection changes.

The Basic Syntax: Unveiling the Power of v-for

The basic syntax for using v-for is as follows:

```
        <ul>
    <li v-for="item in items" :key="item.id">{{ item.name
}}</li>
</ul>
```

Let's break down this syntax:

- **item**: This is the alias for the current item being iterated over in the items array. You can choose any valid variable name for item.
- **items**: This is the array (or object) that you want to iterate over. It should be a data property in your Vue instance.
- **in**: This is the keyword that connects the item alias to the items array.
- **:key="item.id"**: This is the *crucial* key attribute. We'll discuss its importance in detail later.
- **{{ item.name }}**: This is the content that will be rendered for each item in the array. In this example, we're displaying the name property of each item.

Accessing the Index: Knowing Your Position in the List

In addition to the item itself, you can also access the index (position) of the item in the array using the following syntax:

```
<ul>
  <li v-for="(item, index) in items" :key="item.id">{{ index + 1 }}. {{ item.name }}</li>
</ul>
```

Here, index represents the current position of the item in the array, starting from 0. We add 1 to index to display the item number starting from 1 instead of 0.

Iterating Over Objects: Beyond Arrays

v-for isn't limited to iterating over arrays. You can also use it to iterate over the properties of an object.

```
<ul>
  <li v-for="(value, key, index) in myObject" :key="key">{{ index + 1 }}. {{ key }}: {{ value }}</li>
</ul>
```

In this case:

- value: Represents the value of the property.
- key: Represents the name of the property.

- index: Represents the position of the property in the object (starting from 0).

Important Note: When iterating over objects, the order of properties is *not guaranteed* to be consistent across browsers. If you need a specific order, you should convert the object to an array of key-value pairs and iterate over the array instead.

The :key Attribute: The Cornerstone of Efficient List Rendering

The :key attribute is *essential* when using v-for. It provides Vue.js with a unique identifier for each item in the list. This allows Vue.js to efficiently track changes in the list and update the DOM correctly.

Why is :key So Important?

Vue.js uses a virtual DOM to optimize DOM updates. When the data changes, Vue.js creates a virtual representation of the DOM and compares it to the real DOM. It then only updates the parts of the real DOM that have changed.

The key attribute helps Vue.js identify which elements in the virtual DOM correspond to which elements in the real DOM. Without a key, Vue.js has to re-render the entire list whenever the data changes, which can be very inefficient.

Choosing the Right key Value:

- **Use a Unique and Stable Identifier:** The ideal key value is a unique and stable identifier for each item in the list, such as an ID from a database.

```
<li v-for="item in items" :key="item.id">{{ item.name }}</li>
```

- **Avoid Using the Index as the key (Unless Necessary):** In some cases, you might not have a unique and stable identifier for each item. In these cases, you can use the index as the key, but be aware that this can lead to performance issues if the list is frequently reordered.

```
<li v-for="(item, index) in items" :key="index">{{ item.name }}</li>
```

When is it okay to use the index? It's generally acceptable to use the index when:

- The list is static (never changes).
- The list is only ever appended to (items are only added to the end).
- You are only displaying data and not using any interactive elements within the list items (e.g., input fields, buttons).

If any of these conditions are not met, it's best to find a more stable and unique identifier for the key.

The <template> Element and v-for: Rendering Multiple Elements Without a Wrapper

Similar to v-if, you can use the <template> element with v-for to render multiple elements for each item in the list without creating a wrapper element.

```
<ul>
  <template v-for="item in items" :key="item.id">
    <li>{{ item.name }}</li>
    <p>{{ item.description }}</p>
  </template>
</ul>
```

This will generate a <li> and a <p> element for each item in the items array, without creating an extra <div> or other wrapper element around them.

Filtering and Sorting Lists: Leveraging Computed Properties

Often, you'll need to display a filtered or sorted version of a list. While you *could* perform the filtering or sorting directly within the v-for loop, it's generally best to use a computed property instead.

```
const { createApp } = Vue;

const app = createApp({
  data() {
    return {
      items: [
```

```
        { id: 1, name: 'Apple', price: 1.00, category:
'Fruit' },
        { id: 2, name: 'Banana', price: 0.50, category:
'Fruit' },
        { id: 3, name: 'Carrot', price: 0.75, category:
'Vegetable' }
      ],
      filterCategory: 'All'
    };
  },
  computed: {
    filteredItems() {
      if (this.filterCategory === 'All') {
        return this.items;
      } else {
        return this.items.filter(item => item.category ===
this.filterCategory);
      }
    }
  }
});
```

```
      <ul>
  <li v-for="item in filteredItems" :key="item.id">{{
item.name }}</li>
</ul>
```

This approach offers several benefits:

- **Improved Performance:** The filtering or sorting is only performed when the data changes, not every time the component re-renders.
- **Improved Readability:** The template is cleaner and easier to understand.
- **Improved Testability:** The filtering or sorting logic can be easily tested in isolation.

Practical Example: Building a Dynamic To-Do List

Let's create a practical example that demonstrates the use of v-for in a dynamic to-do list:

```
      <!DOCTYPE html>
<html>
<head>
  <title>To-Do List</title>
  <script
src="https://unpkg.com/vue@3/dist/vue.global.js"></script>
```

```
</head>
<body>
  <div id="app">
    <h1>To-Do List</h1>
    <input type="text" v-model.trim="newTodo"
@keyup.enter="addTodo" placeholder="Add a to-do...">
    <ul>
      <li v-for="todo in todos" :key="todo.id">
        {{ todo.text }}
        <button @click="removeTodo(todo.id)">Remove</button>
      </li>
    </ul>
  </div>

  <script>
    const { createApp } = Vue;

    const app = createApp({
      data() {
        return {
          newTodo: '',
          todos: []
        };
      },
      methods: {
        addTodo() {
          if (this.newTodo.trim() !== '') {
            this.todos.push({ id: Date.now(), text:
this.newTodo });
            this.newTodo = '';
          }
        },
        removeTodo(id) {
          this.todos = this.todos.filter(todo => todo.id !==
id);
        }
      }
    });

    app.mount('#app');
  </script>
</body>
</html>
```

In this example, we use v-for to display a list of to-do items. We use v-model to bind the input field to the newTodo property, and we use @keyup.enter to call the addTodo method when the Enter key is pressed. We also use @click to call the removeTodo method when the "Remove" button is clicked.

Personal Insight: The Power of Iteration

When I first started using v-for, I was amazed at how easily I could display complex lists of data. It saved me so much time and effort compared to manually creating the HTML elements. It's one of the features that makes Vue.js such a productive framework.

Conclusion: Becoming a v-for Master

Mastering v-for is essential for building dynamic and data-driven Vue.js applications. By understanding the syntax, the importance of the :key attribute, and the best practices for filtering and sorting lists, you can efficiently and effectively display collections of data in your user interfaces. In the next section, we'll explore Event Handling, where we will see how we can make our app do things.

2.4 Event Handling (v-on): Responding to User Interactions – Making Your App React to the World

Event handling is what brings your web applications to life. It's the mechanism that allows your app to respond to user actions like clicks, keystrokes, mouse movements, and form submissions. Without event handling, your app would be a static display, unresponsive to the user's input. Vue.js provides the v-on directive (and its convenient shorthand, @) to make event handling intuitive and powerful.

Think of event handling as setting up listening posts within your application. You tell Vue.js to "listen" for specific events on certain elements. When those events occur, Vue.js triggers the corresponding methods in your Vue instance, allowing you to react to the user's actions and update the application's state.

The Basic Syntax: Connecting Events to Methods

The basic syntax for using v-on is as follows:

```
<button v-on:click="handleClick">Click Me</button>
```

Let's break down this syntax:

- **v-on:click**: This specifies the event you want to listen for. In this case, it's the click event. You can listen for a wide range of DOM events, such as mouseover, keyup, submit, and many more.
- **handleClick**: This is the name of the method in your Vue instance that you want to call when the click event occurs.

The @ Shorthand: A Quick and Clean Alternative

Vue.js provides a shorthand notation for v-on using the @ symbol:

```
<button @click="handleClick">Click Me</button>
```

This shorthand is functionally equivalent to v-on:click, but it's more concise and easier to read. You'll likely find yourself using the @ shorthand most of the time.

Defining Event Handlers: The methods Option

Event handlers are methods defined within the methods option of your Vue instance. These methods are responsible for responding to the events that you're listening for.

```
const { createApp } = Vue;

const app = createApp({
  data() {
    return {
      count: 0
    };
  },
  methods: {
    handleClick() {
      this.count++;
    }
  }
});
```

In this example, the handleClick method is called when the button is clicked. The method increments the count data property, which will then be reflected in the template due to Vue's reactivity system.

Accessing the Vue Instance: The this Keyword

Within your event handlers, you can access the Vue instance using the this keyword. This allows you to access and modify the data properties, call other methods, and interact with the component's state.

Passing Arguments to Event Handlers: Adding Context to Your Actions

You can pass arguments to your event handlers from the template. This allows you to provide additional context to the method, such as the ID of an item to be deleted or the value of an input field.

```
    <button @click="removeItem(item.id)">Remove</button>

    methods: {
  removeItem(itemId) {
    // Remove the item with the given ID
  }
}
```

In this example, the removeItem method receives the item.id as an argument.

Accessing the Native DOM Event: The $event Object

Sometimes, you need to access the native DOM event object within your event handler. This object provides information about the event that occurred, such as the target element, the mouse coordinates, or the key that was pressed. You can access the $event object by passing it as an argument to your event handler in the template.

```
    <button @click="handleClick($event)">Click Me</button>

    methods: {
  handleClick(event) {
    console.log(event.target); // Access the button element
    console.log(event.clientX, event.clientY); // Mouse
coordinates
  }
}
```

Event Modifiers: Streamlining Common Tasks

Vue.js provides event modifiers that simplify common tasks like preventing the default event behavior or stopping event propagation. These modifiers are added as suffixes to the event name in the template.

- **.prevent**: Prevents the default event behavior (e.g., preventing a form from submitting).

```
<form @submit.prevent="handleSubmit">
  <!-- Form content -->
</form>
```

- **.stop**: Stops event propagation (prevents the event from bubbling up the DOM tree).

```
<div @click="outerDivClick">
  <button @click.stop="innerButtonClick">Click Me</button>
</div>
```

In this example, clicking the button will only trigger the innerButtonClick method, not the outerDivClick method.

- **.self**: Only triggers the handler if the event was dispatched from the element itself.

```
<div @click.self="divClick">
  <!-- Content -->
</div>
```

The divClick method will only be triggered if the user clicks directly on the div element, not on any of its children.

- **.capture**: Uses the capture mode when adding the event listener.
- **.once**: The event handler will be invoked at most once.
- **.passive**: Indicates that the event listener will not call preventDefault(). This can improve scrolling performance.

Keyboard Event Modifiers: Reacting to Specific Keys

Vue.js also provides keyboard event modifiers that allow you to listen for specific keys being pressed.

```
<input type="text" @keyup.enter="submitForm"> <!--
Enter key -->
<input type="text" @keyup.esc="cancelForm">   <!-- Escape key
-->
```

You can also use system modifier keys (Ctrl, Alt, Shift, Meta):

```
<input type="text" @keyup.ctrl.enter="saveForm"> <!--
Ctrl + Enter -->
```

Practical Example: Building a Simple Counter

Let's create a practical example that demonstrates the use of event handling to build a simple counter:

```
<!DOCTYPE html>
<html>
<head>
  <title>Simple Counter</title>
  <script
src="https://unpkg.com/vue@3/dist/vue.global.js"></script>
</head>
<body>
  <div id="app">
    <h1>Count: {{ count }}</h1>
    <button @click="increment">Increment</button>
    <button @click="decrement">Decrement</button>
  </div>

  <script>
    const { createApp } = Vue;

    const app = createApp({
      data() {
        return {
          count: 0
        };
      },
      methods: {
        increment() {
          this.count++;
        },
        decrement() {
          this.count--;
        }
      }
    });

    app.mount('#app');
  </script>
</body>
```

```
</html>
```

In this example, we use event handling to increment or decrement the count data property when the corresponding buttons are clicked.

Personal Insight: The Joy of Interactivity

Event handling is what makes web development so exciting! Seeing your app respond to user actions in real-time is incredibly rewarding. It's like giving your creation a mind of its own.

Conclusion: Becoming an Event Handling Expert

Mastering event handling is crucial for building dynamic and interactive Vue.js applications. By understanding the syntax of v-on (and its @ shorthand), the role of the methods option, and the power of event modifiers, you can create applications that respond intelligently to user input. In the next chapter, we will explore Form Input Binding.

2.5 Form Input Binding (v-model): Two-Way Magic – Connecting Your Data to Forms

Forms are a fundamental part of almost every web application. They allow users to input data, which your application can then process and use. Handling forms traditionally involves a lot of manual DOM manipulation to keep the input fields synchronized with the application's data. Vue.js simplifies this process dramatically with the v-model directive, enabling two-way data binding between form input elements and your Vue instance.

Think of v-model as a magic cable that connects your data directly to the user interface. When the user types something into an input field, the corresponding data property in your Vue instance is automatically updated. Conversely, when the data property changes, the input field is automatically updated to reflect the new value. This eliminates the need for manual event listeners and DOM manipulation, making form handling incredibly simple and efficient.

The Basic Syntax: The Power of v-model

The basic syntax for using v-model is as follows:

```
<input type="text" v-model="message">
```

In this example, the v-model directive is bound to the message data property in your Vue instance. Whenever the user types something into the input field, the message property is automatically updated to reflect the new value. Similarly, if you programmatically change the value of the message property in your Vue instance, the input field will be automatically updated to display the new value.

Under the Hood: How v-model Works

v-model is essentially syntactic sugar for a combination of two things:

1. Binding the value attribute of the input element using v-bind (or :).
2. Listening for the input event and updating the data property accordingly.

So, the v-model directive in the previous example is roughly equivalent to:

```
<input
  type="text"
  :value="message"
  @input="message = $event.target.value"
>
```

While this manual approach works, v-model significantly simplifies the code and makes it easier to read and maintain.

v-model with Different Input Types: Adapting to Various Form Elements

v-model adapts its behavior based on the type of input element it's bound to. Let's explore how it works with different form elements:

- **Text Input (<input type="text">, <textarea>):** As we've seen, v-model directly binds to the value property and the input event.

```
<input type="text" v-model="name" placeholder="Your
Name">
<textarea v-model="description"></textarea>
```

- **Checkboxes (<input type="checkbox">):**
    - **Single Checkbox:** When v-model is used with a single checkbox, it binds to the checked attribute. The data property will be a boolean value (true if the checkbox is checked, false if it's not).

```
<input type="checkbox" v-model="agreeTerms">
<label for="agreeTerms">I agree to the terms and
conditions.</label>
```

    - **Multiple Checkboxes:** When v-model is used with multiple checkboxes bound to the same data property (which should be an array), it adds or removes the checkbox's value from the array.

```
<input type="checkbox" value="apple" v-
model="selectedFruits"> Apple
<input type="checkbox" value="banana" v-
model="selectedFruits"> Banana
<input type="checkbox" value="orange" v-
model="selectedFruits"> Orange
```

    If the user checks "apple" and "banana", the selectedFruits array will be ['apple', 'banana'].

- **Radio Buttons (<input type="radio">):** v-model binds to the value attribute. Only one radio button in a group can be selected at a time. The data property will hold the value of the selected radio button.

```
<input type="radio" value="male" v-model="gender"> Male
<input type="radio" value="female" v-model="gender"> Female
<input type="radio" value="other" v-model="gender"> Other
```

- **Select Boxes (<select>):** v-model binds to the selected value of the <select> element.

```
<select v-model="selectedOption">
  <option value="option1">Option 1</option>
  <option value="option2">Option 2</option>
  <option value="option3">Option 3</option>
</select>
```

If the user selects "Option 2", the selectedOption property will be set to "option2".

v-model Modifiers: Fine-Tuning the Binding

v-model provides modifiers that allow you to fine-tune the binding behavior:

- **.lazy**: Updates the data only after a "change" event (when the input loses focus). This is useful for reducing the number of updates and improving performance, especially for complex input fields.

```
<input type="text" v-model.lazy="message">
```

- **.number**: Automatically converts the input value to a number. This is useful for ensuring that the data property is always a number, even if the user enters text.

```
<input type="number" v-model.number="age">
```

- **.trim**: Automatically trims whitespace from the input value. This is useful for preventing leading or trailing spaces from being stored in the data property.

```
<input type="text" v-model.trim="username">
```

Practical Example: Building a Simple Form

Let's create a practical example that demonstrates the use of v-model to build a simple form:

```
<!DOCTYPE html>
<html>
<head>
  <title>Simple Form</title>
  <script
src="https://unpkg.com/vue@3/dist/vue.global.js"></script>
</head>
<body>
  <div id="app">
    <h1>Simple Form</h1>
    <form @submit.prevent="handleSubmit">
      <label for="name">Name:</label>
```

```
      <input type="text" id="name" v-
model.trim="form.name"><br><br>

      <label for="email">Email:</label>
      <input type="email" id="email" v-
model.trim="form.email"><br><br>

      <label for="age">Age:</label>
      <input type="number" id="age" v-
model.number="form.age"><br><br>

      <label for="gender">Gender:</label><br>
      <input type="radio" id="male" value="male" v-
model="form.gender">
      <label for="male">Male</label>
      <input type="radio" id="female" value="female" v-
model="form.gender">
      <label for="female">Female</label><br><br>

      <label for="agree">
        <input type="checkbox" id="agree" v-
model="form.agree">
        I agree to the terms and conditions.
      </label><br><br>

      <button type="submit">Submit</button>
    </form>

    <h2>Form Data:</h2>
    <pre>{{ form }}</pre>
  </div>

  <script>
    const { createApp } = Vue;

    const app = createApp({
      data() {
        return {
          form: {
            name: '',
            email: '',
            age: null,
            gender: null,
            agree: false
          }
        };
      },
      methods: {
        handleSubmit() {
          alert('Form submitted!');
          console.log(this.form);
```

```
            }
        }
    });

    app.mount('#app');
  </script>
</body>
</html>
```

In this example, we use v-model to bind various input elements to the properties of the form data property. The handleSubmit method is called when the form is submitted (using the @submit.prevent event handler to prevent the default form submission behavior). The form data is then logged to the console. The pre tag displays the form data in a readable format.

Personal Insight: The End of Manual Form Handling

Before I discovered v-model, I dreaded working with forms. I had to write a lot of boilerplate code to keep the input fields synchronized with the application's data. v-model completely changed the game for me. It made form handling so much easier and more enjoyable.

Conclusion: Mastering Form Input Binding

v-model is a powerful tool that simplifies form handling in Vue.js. By understanding how it works with different input types and by leveraging its modifiers, you can create dynamic and interactive forms with ease. This frees you from the tedious task of manual DOM manipulation, allowing you to focus on the more exciting aspects of building your applications. In the next section, we will explore Directive Modifiers, a more in depth dive.

2.6 Directive Modifiers: Fine-Tuning Your Directives – Adding Precision to Your Templates

We've explored various directives like v-if, v-show, v-for, v-bind, v-on, and v-model. What makes these directives even more potent are *modifiers*. Directive modifiers are special suffixes denoted by a dot (.) that you can append to a directive to alter its behavior in specific ways. They provide a concise and elegant way to enhance the functionality of your directives without writing additional code.

Think of modifiers as adding optional features to your directives, like adding attachments to an email. They allow you to tailor the behavior of a directive to fit your specific needs, making your templates more expressive and efficient.

Understanding the Concept: Modifying Default Behavior

Modifiers fundamentally alter the *default* behavior of a directive. For example, the default behavior of an @submit event is to refresh the page; .prevent modifies that, stopping the refresh.

Event Modifiers: Enhancing Event Handling

Event modifiers are used with the v-on directive (or its shorthand, @) to modify how events are handled. Let's revisit some key event modifiers:

- **.stop (Stop Propagation):** Prevents the event from bubbling up the DOM tree. This means the event will not trigger any event listeners on parent elements.

```
<div @click="outerDivClick">
  <button @click.stop="innerButtonClick">Click Me</button>
</div>
```

  In this example, clicking the button will only trigger the innerButtonClick method. The outerDivClick method will *not* be triggered because the .stop modifier prevents the click event from bubbling up to the div element.

- **.prevent (Prevent Default):** Prevents the default behavior of the event. This is commonly used with form submissions to prevent the page from refreshing.

```
<form @submit.prevent="handleSubmit">
  <!-- Form content -->
</form>
```

  Without the .prevent modifier, the form would submit and refresh the page, potentially losing any data the user has entered.

- **.self (Self-Only):** Only triggers the handler if the event was dispatched from the element itself. This is useful for preventing events from being triggered by child elements.

```
<div @click.self="divClick">
  <!-- Content -->
</div>
```

The divClick method will only be triggered if the user clicks directly on the div element, not on any of its children.

- **.capture (Capture Mode):** Uses the capture mode when adding the event listener. In capture mode, the event listener is triggered before any event listeners on child elements. This is useful for intercepting events before they reach their intended target.
- **.once (Trigger Once):** The event handler will be invoked at most once. After the first invocation, the event listener is automatically removed.

```
<button @click.once="showGreeting">Show
Greeting</button>
```

The showGreeting method will only be called the first time the button is clicked. Subsequent clicks will have no effect.

- **.passive (Passive Listener):** Indicates that the event listener will not call preventDefault(). This can improve scrolling performance, especially on touch devices. Browsers can optimize scrolling if they know the event listener won't prevent the default scrolling behavior.

```
<div @scroll.passive="handleScroll">
  <!-- Scrollable content -->
</div>
```

Important: Using .passive means you *cannot* call preventDefault() inside the handleScroll method.

Keyboard Event Modifiers: Targeting Specific Key Presses

Vue.js provides modifiers to target specific keys with @keyup and @keydown:

```
<input type="text" @keyup.enter="submitForm">  <!--
Triggers on Enter key -->
<input type="text" @keyup.esc="cancelForm">   <!-- Triggers
on Escape key -->
```

You can also combine keyboard modifiers with system modifiers like ctrl, alt, shift, and meta:

```
<input type="text" @keyup.ctrl.enter="saveForm"> <!--
Triggers only on Ctrl+Enter -->
```

v-model Modifiers: Controlling Data Binding

v-model modifiers alter how input is bound to the data. Let's revisit them:

- **.lazy (Update on Change):** Updates the data only after a "change" event (when the input loses focus).

  ```
  <input type="text" v-model.lazy="message">
  ```

  This is useful for reducing the number of updates and improving performance, especially when users are typing rapidly.

- **.number (Convert to Number):** Automatically converts the input value to a number.

  ```
  <input type="number" v-model.number="age">
  ```

  If the user enters a non-numeric value, it will be parsed as NaN.

- **.trim (Trim Whitespace):** Automatically trims whitespace from the input value.

  ```
  <input type="text" v-model.trim="username">
  ```

  This prevents leading or trailing spaces from being stored in the data property.

Important Notes:

- **Modifier Order Matters (Sometimes):** The order of modifiers can sometimes be important. For example, @click.prevent.self is different from @click.self.prevent. In the former, prevent is executed *before* the self check, while in the latter, self is checked *before* prevent is executed.
- **Not All Directives Have Modifiers:** Only certain directives support modifiers. It's always best to consult the Vue.js documentation to see which modifiers are available for a given directive.
- **Custom Directives (A Teaser):** You can even define your own modifiers when creating custom directives (we'll explore custom directives later).

Practical Example: A More Robust Form

Let's enhance our simple form example from the previous section with some directive modifiers:

```
      <!DOCTYPE html>
<html>
<head>
  <title>Form with Modifiers</title>
  <script
src="https://unpkg.com/vue@3/dist/vue.global.js"></script>
</head>
<body>
  <div id="app">
    <h1>Form with Modifiers</h1>
    <form @submit.prevent="handleSubmit">
      <label for="name">Name:</label>
      <input type="text" id="name" v-
model.trim="form.name"><br><br>

      <label for="email">Email:</label>
      <input type="email" id="email" v-
model.trim="form.email"><br><br>

      <label for="age">Age:</label>
      <input type="number" id="age" v-
model.number="form.age"><br><br>

      <label for="message">Message:</label>
      <textarea id="message" v-
model.lazy="form.message"></textarea><br><br>

      <button type="submit">Submit</button>
```

```
    </form>

    <h2>Form Data:</h2>
    <pre>{{ form }}</pre>
  </div>

  <script>
    const { createApp } = Vue;

    const app = createApp({
      data() {
        return {
          form: {
            name: '',
            email: '',
            age: null,
            message: ''
          }
        };
      },
      methods: {
        handleSubmit() {
          alert('Form submitted!');
          console.log(this.form);
        }
      }
    });

    app.mount('#app');
  </script>
</body>
</html>
```

Enhancements:

- v-model.trim is used on the name and email input fields to automatically trim whitespace.
- v-model.number is used on the age input field to ensure the age is a number.
- v-model.lazy is used on the message textarea to update the data only when the textarea loses focus.

Personal Insight: Discovering the Power of .prevent

I distinctly remember the first time I used the .prevent modifier. Before that, I was manually calling event.preventDefault() in my event handlers, which felt cumbersome and repetitive. The .prevent modifier simplified my code and made it much more readable.

Conclusion: Mastering Directive Modifiers

Directive modifiers are powerful tools for fine-tuning the behavior of your directives in Vue.js. By understanding the available modifiers and how they work, you can create more expressive, efficient, and maintainable templates. Remember to consult the Vue.js documentation for a complete list of available modifiers and their specific usage. This concludes our exploration into Templates, congratulations on expanding your knowledge.

Chapter 3: Building with Components – The Foundation of Reusable UI

Welcome to the world of components! In the previous chapters, we've covered the fundamentals of Vue.js, including template syntax, directives, and event handling. Now, it's time to take your Vue.js skills to the next level by exploring components.

Components are the building blocks of modern web applications. They allow you to break down complex UIs into smaller, reusable, and manageable pieces. Think of components as Lego bricks: each brick has a specific purpose, and you can combine them in various ways to create complex structures.

Mastering components is essential for building scalable, maintainable, and testable Vue.js applications. They promote code reuse, improve organization, and make it easier to collaborate with other developers. So, let's dive in and discover the power of components!

3.1 What are Components? – Understanding the Core Concept

At the heart of any robust Vue.js application lies the concept of components. They're not just a feature; they're a fundamental design pattern, a way of thinking about building UIs that promotes reusability, maintainability, and testability.

In essence, a component is a self-contained, reusable unit of code that encapsulates a specific part of your user interface. It's like a mini-application within your larger Vue.js application, with its own template (HTML structure), script (JavaScript logic), and optionally, styles (CSS). The best way to think of a component is a custom HTML element.

Components allow us to split our application into small parts, and reason about them independently, rather than having to manage a big monolithic codebase.

Components as Reusable Building Blocks:

Imagine building with Lego bricks. Each brick has a specific shape and purpose. You can combine these bricks in various ways to build different structures, from simple houses to complex castles.

Vue.js components are like Lego bricks for your user interface. You can create components for buttons, input fields, navigation bars, product listings, and any other UI element you can imagine. Once you've created a component, you can reuse it multiple times throughout your application, saving you from writing the same code over and over again.

Benefits of Using Components – Why Embrace the Component Mindset?

The advantages of using components are manifold. Embracing the component mindset leads to:

- **Enhanced Reusability:** Components can be used repeatedly across your project.
    - *Example:* A button component, styled in a particular way, can be used in multiple forms, navigation menus, and modal dialogs, ensuring consistency across your interface.
- **Improved Maintainability:** Components create a modular codebase
    - *Example:* When design or functionality requirements change, modular components prevent cascading, difficult-to-trace bugs.
- **Increased Testability:** Components that are well isolated can be tested with ease.
    - *Example:* You can write unit tests specifically to ensure that a certain search component is returning values correctly.
- **Collaboration Facilitation:** Teams can divide work based on components.
    - *Example:* One developer can take care of the header, while another one is creating the footer.
- **Overall code Organization:** A component based architecture helps divide complexity into maintainable chunks.

Analogy: From Monolith to Modularity

Imagine you're building a complex machine. You could try to assemble it all at once, connecting every wire and bolt without any clear plan. This would be incredibly difficult, time-consuming, and error-prone.

Alternatively, you could break the machine down into smaller, self-contained modules, each with a specific function. You could then assemble these modules together to create the final machine. This approach would be much easier, more organized, and less prone to errors.

Vue.js components allow you to build your web applications in a similar way. By breaking your UI into smaller, self-contained components, you can manage the complexity of your application and build it more efficiently.

Personal Experience: The "Aha!" Moment

I recall the moment when the concept of components truly clicked for me. I was working on a large project with a complex user interface. The codebase was becoming increasingly difficult to manage, and making even small changes felt like a risky operation.

Then, I started to refactor the application using components. I broke down the UI into smaller, self-contained units, each with its own responsibilities. Suddenly, the codebase became much more manageable, and making changes became much easier. It was like a weight had been lifted off my shoulders.

What's Inside a Component? – The Key Ingredients

A Vue.js component typically consists of three key ingredients:

- **Template:** The HTML structure that defines the component's visual appearance. This is where you use Vue.js's template syntax to bind data to the DOM, conditionally render elements, and handle events.
- **Script:** The JavaScript logic that controls the component's behavior. This includes defining data properties, computed properties, methods, and lifecycle hooks.
- **Style (Optional):** The CSS styles that define the component's visual styling. You can use scoped styles to limit the styles to the component itself, or you can use global styles that apply to the entire application.

A Simple Example: Building a Reusable Button

Let's create a simple example of a reusable button component:

```
Vue.component('my-button', {
```

```
  template: `
    <button class="my-button">
      {{ label }}
    </button>
  `,
  props: {
    label: {
      type: String,
      default: 'Click Me'
    }
  },
  style: `.my-button {
    background-color: #4CAF50; /* Green */
    border: none;
    color: white;
    padding: 15px 32px;
    text-align: center;
    text-decoration: none;
    display: inline-block;
    font-size: 16px;
    cursor: pointer;
  }`
});
```

In this example, we define a global component named my-button. The component has a template that defines the HTML structure of the button, a props option that defines the label prop, and a style option that defines the CSS styles for the button.

We can now use this component multiple times throughout our application:

```
      <div id="app">
  <my-button label="Submit"></my-button>
  <my-button label="Cancel"></my-button>
  <my-button></my-button>
</div>
```

This will render three buttons with different labels. The third button will use the default label "Click Me".

Key Takeaways:

- Components are reusable UI elements that encapsulate their own template, script, and style.

- Components promote code reuse, improve maintainability, and make it easier to collaborate with other developers.
- Understanding components is essential for building scalable, testable and maintainable Vue.js applications.

This simple example demonstrates the power of components. By encapsulating the button's HTML, JavaScript, and CSS into a single unit, we can easily reuse the button throughout our application, ensuring a consistent look and feel.

Conclusion: Embracing the Component-Based Future

Components are the foundation of modern web development, and Vue.js makes it incredibly easy to build and use them. By embracing the component mindset, you can create more organized, maintainable, and scalable applications. In the following sections, we'll explore how to register components, pass data to them, and communicate between them. Get ready to unlock the full potential of Vue.js!

3.2 Creating Global and Local Components – Defining Your Building Blocks

Now that we understand *what* components are, let's learn *how* to create them. In Vue.js, you have two primary ways to register your components: globally and locally. Choosing the right registration method is key to organizing your project and ensuring code clarity. It's like deciding whether to put tools in a shared garage or a dedicated toolbox.

Global Components: Universally Accessible Building Blocks

Global components, as the name suggests, are registered directly with the Vue application instance, making them available for use in *any* template within that application. Once registered, you can use them just like you'd use native HTML elements, anywhere within your Vue app.

To register a global component, you use the component() method of the Vue application instance:

```
    const { createApp } = Vue;

const app = createApp({});
```

```
app.component('MyGlobalComponent', {
  template: '<div>This is a global component!</div>'
});

app.mount('#app');
```

Dissecting the Code:

1. const { createApp } = Vue; - Imports the createApp function from the Vue library.
2. const app = createApp({}); - Creates a new Vue application instance. This is the foundation of your Vue app.
3. app.component('MyGlobalComponent', { ... }); - Registers the component. This is the key part!
    - 'MyGlobalComponent' is the name of your component. This is the tag name you'll use in your templates (e.g., <my-global-component>). Vue recommends using kebab-case for component names.
    - { ... } is the component definition object. This object contains all the options that define the component's behavior and appearance (template, data, methods, props, etc.).
4. template: '<div>This is a global component!</div>' defines the HTML structure of the component. This is the content that will be rendered when you use the component in your template.

Using a Global Component:

Once you've registered a global component, you can use it in any template within your application, just like you would use a regular HTML element:

```
    <div id="app">
  <MyGlobalComponent></MyGlobalComponent>
</div>
```

Benefits of Global Components:

- **Convenience:** You don't need to import or register them in every component where you want to use them.
- **Accessibility:** They're available throughout your entire application.

Drawbacks of Global Components:

- **Namespace Pollution:** They can pollute the global namespace, making it harder to track which components are being used where.
- **Implicit Dependencies:** It's not always clear which components a particular component depends on. This can make it harder to maintain and refactor your code.
- **Larger Initial Bundle:** All global components are included in the initial bundle, even if they aren't used on the first page load. This can increase the initial load time of your application.

Local Components: Encapsulated Building Blocks

Local components, on the other hand, are registered within a specific component. This means they're only available for use in that component and its child components. They provide better encapsulation and help to prevent namespace pollution.

To register a local component, you include it in the components option of a Vue component:

```
      const { createApp } = Vue;

const MyLocalComponent = {
  template: '<div>This is a local component!</div>'
};

const app = createApp({
  components: {
    MyLocalComponent
  },
  template: `
    <div>
      <MyLocalComponent></MyLocalComponent>
    </div>
  `
});

app.mount('#app');
```

Dissecting the Code:

1. const MyLocalComponent = { ... }; - Defines the component as a JavaScript object.
2. components: { MyLocalComponent } - Registers the component locally.

- MyLocalComponent (key) is the component name you'll use in the template (e.g., <my-local-component>). This uses ES6 shorthand; it's equivalent to MyLocalComponent: MyLocalComponent.

Using a Local Component:

You can now use the MyLocalComponent in the template of the component where it's registered:

```
    <div id="app">
  <MyLocalComponent></MyLocalComponent>
</div>
```

Benefits of Local Components:

- **Better Encapsulation:** Local components are only available within the component where they're registered, preventing namespace pollution and reducing the risk of naming conflicts.
- **Explicit Dependencies:** It's clear which components a particular component depends on. This makes it easier to maintain and refactor your code.
- **Smaller Bundle Size:** Only the components that are used on a particular page are included in the initial bundle, reducing the initial load time of your application.

Drawbacks of Local Components:

- **More Verbose:** You need to import and register them in every component where you want to use them, which can be more verbose.

Personal Insight: The Global vs. Local Revelation

When I first started with Vue.js, I was tempted to register all my components globally for convenience. However, as my projects grew in size and complexity, I quickly realized the limitations of this approach. I started to embrace local components and found that they significantly improved the organization and maintainability of my code.

Global vs. Local: Choosing the Right Approach – A Guiding Principle

Here's a guiding principle for choosing between global and local components:

- **Start with Local Components:** By default, prefer local components for most of your UI elements. This promotes better encapsulation and reduces the risk of naming conflicts.
- **Use Global Components Sparingly:** Reserve global components for elements that are used throughout your *entire* application, such as layout components (e.g., a header, a footer, or a sidebar) or utility components (e.g., a reusable button or a date picker).

A Complete Example: Global and Local Harmony

Let's create a complete example that demonstrates the use of both global and local components:

```
      <!DOCTYPE html>
<html>
<head>
  <title>Global and Local Components</title>
  <script
src="https://unpkg.com/vue@3/dist/vue.global.js"></script>
</head>
<body>
  <div id="app">
    <my-header></my-header>  <!-- Global component -->
    <my-content></my-content> <!-- Root component with local
components -->
    <my-footer></my-footer>  <!-- Global component -->
  </div>

  <script>
    const { createApp } = Vue;

    // Global component
    const MyHeader = {
      template: '<h1>My Awesome App</h1>'
    };

    // Global component
    const MyFooter = {
      template: '<p>Copyright 2023</p>'
    };

    // Local component
    const MyArticle = {
      template: '<article>This is an article.</article>'
    };
```

```
    const app = createApp({
      components: {
        MyArticle // Local component
      },
      template: `
        <div>
          <MyArticle></MyArticle>
        </div>
      `
    });

    app.component('MyHeader', MyHeader); // Register global
    app.component('MyFooter', MyFooter); // Register global

    app.mount('#app');
  </script>
</body>
</html>
```

Explanation:

1. **Global Components:** MyHeader and MyFooter are registered globally, making them available throughout the application.
2. **Local Component:** MyArticle is registered locally within the root component.
3. **Template:** The root component's template uses both the global and local components.

This example demonstrates how to use both global and local components in a Vue.js application.

Key Takeaways:

- Global components are registered with the Vue application instance and are available throughout the application.
- Local components are registered within a specific component and are only available in that component and its children.
- Use local components by default to promote better encapsulation and reduce the risk of naming conflicts.
- Reserve global components for elements that are used throughout your entire application.

Conclusion: Defining Your Building Blocks with Confidence

Understanding the difference between global and local components is crucial for building well-organized and maintainable Vue.js applications. By choosing the right registration method for each component, you can create a codebase that is easy to understand, debug, and refactor. This foundational knowledge is essential as we move forward to exploring how to communicate between components using props and events.

3.3 Props: Passing Data to Components – Communicating with Your Building Blocks

Now that we've learned how to create components, it's time to explore how to pass data into them. This is where *props* come in. Props are custom attributes that you can define on a component, allowing you to pass data from a parent component to a child component. Think of them as the input parameters that you provide when you use a function or method.

Props are the primary mechanism for parent components to configure and control the behavior of their child components. They enable you to create reusable components that can be customized with different data, making them more flexible and versatile.

Understanding the Flow: Parent to Child

The flow of data with props is *unidirectional,* meaning data flows from the parent component down to the child component. Child components should *never* directly modify props they receive from their parent. This unidirectional flow helps maintain data integrity and makes it easier to understand how data is changing in your application. We'll explore how child components communicate back to their parents in a later section on events.

Defining Props: Declaring What Your Component Expects

To define props on a component, you use the props option. The props option can be an array of prop names or an object with more detailed configuration options.

1. Array Syntax (Simple but Limited):

```
    Vue.component('my-component', {
props: ['message', 'count', 'isActive'],
```

```
  template: '<div>{{ message }} - {{ count }} - {{ isActive
}}</div>'
});
```

In this example, we declare three props: message, count, and isActive. This is the simplest way to define props, but it doesn't allow you to specify data types or validation rules.

2. Object Syntax (More Powerful and Flexible):

The object syntax provides more control over your props and allows you to specify data types, validation rules, and default values:

```
    Vue.component('my-component', {
  props: {
    message: {
      type: String,
      required: true,
      validator: function (value) {
        return value.length > 10; // Minimum length
      }
    },
    count: {
      type: Number,
      default: 0
    },
    isActive: {
      type: Boolean,
      default: false
    }
  },
  template: '<div>{{ message }} - {{ count }} - {{ isActive
}}</div>'
});
```

Let's break down the object syntax:

- **type:** Specifies the expected data type of the prop. Vue.js supports various data types, including String, Number, Boolean, Array, Object, Date, Function, Symbol, and custom constructor functions.
- **required:** A boolean value that indicates whether the prop is required. If required is set to true and the parent component doesn't provide a value for the prop, Vue.js will issue a warning.

- **default:** Specifies a default value for the prop if the parent component doesn't provide a value. The default value can be a simple value or a function that returns the default value. If the default value is an object or an array, you *must* use a function to return a new instance of the object or array each time the component is created (to avoid sharing the same object or array between multiple component instances).
- **validator:** A function that validates the prop's value. The function receives the prop's value as an argument and should return true if the value is valid or false if it's invalid. Vue.js will issue a warning if the validator returns false.

Passing Props: From Parent to Child

To pass props to a component, you use the same syntax as you would for any other HTML attribute:

```
<my-component message="Hello from the parent!"
count="5" :is-active="true"></my-component>
```

Note the use of : (the shorthand for v-bind) for the isActive prop. This is because we're passing a JavaScript expression (the boolean value true) rather than a literal string. When passing non-string values, you *must* use v-bind (or its shorthand).

Prop Casing (kebab-case vs. camelCase):

When defining props in your component's JavaScript code, you should use camelCase (e.g., myProp). However, when passing props from the parent component in your HTML template, you should use kebab-case (e.g., my-prop). Vue.js automatically handles the conversion between the two casing styles.

Using Props in the Template: Displaying and Manipulating Data

Inside your component's template, you can access the props just like you would access any other data property:

```
<template>
 <div>
  <h1>{{ message }}</h1>
  <p>Count: {{ count }}</p>
```

```
    <p v-if="isActive">This component is active!</p>
  </div>
</template>
```

One-Way Data Flow (Respecting the Parent's Data):

It's crucial to remember that props are *read-only* from the perspective of the child component. You should *never* directly modify a prop within a child component. Doing so violates the one-way data flow principle and can lead to unexpected behavior and debugging headaches.

What to Do If You Need to Modify a Prop:

If you need to modify the data passed in via a prop, there are two common approaches:

1. **Create a Local Data Copy:** Create a local data property in the child component and initialize it with the value of the prop. You can then modify the local data property without affecting the original prop in the parent component.

```
    Vue.component('my-component', {
  props: ['initialCount'],
  data() {
    return {
      count: this.initialCount // Create a local copy
    };
  },
  template: '<div>Count: {{ count }} <button
@click="count++">Increment</button></div>'
});
```

2. **Emit an Event to the Parent:** Emit an event to the parent component, signaling that the data needs to be updated. The parent component can then update the prop, which will be reflected in the child component through the one-way data flow. We'll cover event emission in the next section.

Practical Example: A Customizable Product Card

Let's create a practical example of a customizable product card component that uses props to display product information:

```
<!DOCTYPE html>
<html>
<head>
  <title>Product Card Component</title>
  <script
src="https://unpkg.com/vue@3/dist/vue.global.js"></script>
  <style>
    .product-card {
      border: 1px solid #ccc;
      padding: 10px;
      margin-bottom: 10px;
    }
  </style>
</head>
<body>
  <div id="app">
    <product-card
      :name="product1.name"
      :price="product1.price"
      :description="product1.description"
      :image-url="product1.imageUrl"
    ></product-card>

    <product-card
      :name="product2.name"
      :price="product2.price"
      :description="product2.description"
      :image-url="product2.imageUrl"
    ></product-card>
  </div>

  <script>
    const { createApp } = Vue;

    Vue.component('product-card', {
      props: {
        name: {
          type: String,
          required: true
        },
        price: {
          type: Number,
          required: true
        },
        description: {
          type: String,
          default: ''
        },
        imageUrl: {
          type: String,
          default: 'https://via.placeholder.com/150'
```

```
        }
      },
      template: `
        <div class="product-card">
          <img :src="imageUrl" :alt="name" width="150">
          <h2>{{ name }}</h2>
          <p>Price: ${{ price }}</p>
          <p>{{ description }}</p>
        </div>
      `
    });

    const app = createApp({
      data() {
        return {
          product1: {
            name: 'Awesome Laptop',
            price: 1200,
            description: 'A powerful laptop for all your
needs.',
            imageUrl: 'https://via.placeholder.com/150'
          },
          product2: {
            name: 'Wireless Mouse',
            price: 25,
            description: 'A comfortable and reliable wireless
mouse.'
          }
        };
      }
    });

    app.mount('#app');
  </script>
</body>
</html>
```

In this example, we define a product-card component that accepts name, price, description, and imageUrl props. The parent component passes different data to the product-card component for each product, allowing us to reuse the same component to display different product information.

Personal Insight: The Importance of Prop Validation

I learned the importance of prop validation the hard way. I was working on a project where I accidentally passed the wrong data type to a component's prop. This caused a subtle bug that was difficult to track down. After that experience, I made it a habit to always define prop types and validation rules to catch errors early on.

Conclusion: Mastering Data Communication with Props

Props are the foundation for passing data from parent components to child components in Vue.js. By understanding how to define props, pass data, and respect the one-way data flow, you can create reusable and maintainable components that can be customized with different data. In the next section, we'll explore how child components can communicate back to their parent components using events.

3.4 Emitting Events from Components – Communicating Back to the Parent

While props provide a mechanism for parent components to pass data down to child components, there often arises a need for child components to communicate back to their parents. This is where *events* come into play. In Vue.js, components can emit custom events that parent components can listen for and respond to.

Think of events as messages that a child component sends to its parent to notify it of something that has happened. These messages can carry data, allowing the parent component to update its state or trigger other actions based on the child's activity. This two-way communication is vital for building complex and interactive user interfaces.

The One-Way Data Flow (Still in Control):

Even with event emission, the fundamental principle of one-way data flow remains in effect. The child component *cannot* directly modify the parent's data. Instead, it emits an event to *request* that the parent update its data. This separation of concerns ensures that the parent component retains control over its own state.

Emitting Events: Sending Messages from Child to Parent

To emit an event from a component, you use the $emit() method. The $emit() method takes two arguments:

1. **The event name:** A string that identifies the event.

2. **Optional payload data:** Any data that you want to send along with the event.

```
    Vue.component('my-button', {
  template: '<button @click="handleClick">Click Me</button>',
  methods: {
    handleClick() {
      this.$emit('button-clicked', 'Hello from the button!');
    }
  }
});
```

In this example, the my-button component emits a button-clicked event when the button is clicked. The event also includes a payload of data: the string "Hello from the button!".

Naming Conventions for Events:

It's a common convention to use kebab-case for event names (e.g., button-clicked, item-deleted). This helps to distinguish custom events from native DOM events, which are typically written in lowercase (e.g., click, mouseover).

Listening for Events: The Parent's Response

To listen for an event emitted by a component, you use the v-on directive (or its shorthand, @) on the component's tag in the parent component's template:

```
    <my-button @button-clicked="handleButtonClicked"></my-
button>
```

In this example, the handleButtonClicked method in the parent component will be called when the button-clicked event is emitted by the my-button component.

Accessing the Event Payload: Receiving the Message

You can access the data that was sent along with the event in the parent component's event handler:

```
    Vue.component('my-button', {
  template: '<button @click="handleClick">Click Me</button>',
```

```
  methods: {
    handleClick() {
      this.$emit('button-clicked', 'Hello from the button!');
    }
  }
});

      const { createApp } = Vue;

const app = createApp({
  methods: {
    handleButtonClicked(message) {
      console.log(message); // Output: Hello from the button!
    }
  }
});
```

In this example, the handleButtonClicked method receives the message data that was sent along with the button-clicked event.

The $event Object (A Special Case):

If you need to access the original DOM event object in your parent component's event handler, you can pass the special $event variable to the event handler in the template:

```
      <my-button @click="handleButtonClicked($event)"></my-
button>
```

In this case, the handleButtonClicked method will receive the DOM click event object as its argument. However, be aware that using $event will prevent you from also passing any data emitted by the child. Usually it's best to rely on custom emitted data, not the raw event itself.

A Deprecated Approach: The .sync Modifier (Avoid in Vue 3!)

In Vue 2, there was a .sync modifier that provided a shorthand for automatically updating a prop in the parent component when a specific event was emitted by the child component. However, the .sync modifier has been *deprecated* in Vue 3 and is no longer recommended.

Why .sync is Deprecated:

The .sync modifier made it less clear how data was flowing in the application, making it harder to debug and maintain. It also introduced some ambiguity about which component was responsible for updating the data.

The Recommended Approach (Explicit Event Emission):

The preferred approach in Vue 3 is to emit a custom event and explicitly update the prop in the parent component:

```
    Vue.component('my-component', {
  props: ['count'],
  template: '<div>{{ count }} <button
@click="increment">Increment</button></div>',
  methods: {
    increment() {
      this.$emit('update:count', this.count + 1);
    }
  }
});

    <my-component :count="parentCount"
@update:count="parentCount = $event"></my-component>
```

Dissecting this New Approach:

1. **Props:** We define the props with props: ['count'].
2. **Event:** In this example, the recommended way is to add a "update:" before the original prop name: this.$emit('update:count', this.count + 1);. We still use $emit.
3. **Listening:** In the parent template, we now listen for the new event: @update:count="parentCount = $event".

Practical Example: A Star Rating Component

Let's create a practical example of a star rating component that uses events to communicate the selected rating back to the parent component:

```
    <!DOCTYPE html>
<html>
<head>
  <title>Star Rating Component</title>
  <script
src="https://unpkg.com/vue@3/dist/vue.global.js"></script>
  <style>
    .star {
```

```
      font-size: 24px;
      cursor: pointer;
    }
    .star.active {
      color: gold;
    }
  </style>
</head>
<body>
  <div id="app">
    <h2>Rating: {{ rating }}</h2>
    <star-rating :initial-rating="rating" @rating-
selected="rating = $event"></star-rating>
  </div>

  <script>
    const { createApp } = Vue;

    Vue.component('star-rating', {
      props: {
        initialRating: {
          type: Number,
          default: 0
        }
      },
      data() {
        return {
          rating: this.initialRating
        };
      },
      template: `
        <div>
          <span
            class="star"
            v-for="n in 5"
            :key="n"
            :class="{ active: n <= rating }"
            @click="setRating(n)"
          >★</span>
        </div>
      `,
      methods: {
        setRating(newRating) {
          this.rating = newRating;
          this.$emit('rating-selected', newRating);
        }
      }
    });

    const app = createApp({
      data() {
```

```
        return {
          rating: 3
        };
      }
    });

    app.mount('#app');
  </script>
</body>
</html>
```

Explanation:

1. **Star Rating Component:** The star-rating component displays five stars. Clicking a star sets the component's internal rating data property and emits a rating-selected event with the new rating value.
2. **Parent Component:** The parent component listens for the rating-selected event and updates its own rating data property accordingly.
3. **Unidirectional Flow:** While the star-rating component has its own internal rating value, that value is independent of the parent's rating value.

Personal Insight: Events Enable Complex Interactions

Events are the key to building complex and interactive user interfaces in Vue.js. They allow you to create components that can react to user actions and communicate those actions to other parts of your application.

Conclusion: Mastering Two-Way Communication

Events provide a powerful mechanism for child components to communicate back to their parent components. By understanding how to emit and listen for events, and how to handle event data, you can create highly interactive and dynamic Vue.js applications. In the next section, we'll explore Single-File Components.

3.5 Single-File Components (.vue files) – Organizing Your Code: The SFC Revolution

We've been defining components using JavaScript objects with template, data, methods, and so on. While this works, it quickly becomes unwieldy for larger components. Imagine writing a whole book inside a single HTML tag!

That's where Single-File Components (SFCs), with the .vue extension, come to the rescue. They are a cornerstone of modern Vue.js development, providing a clean, organized, and powerful way to encapsulate a component's logic, template, and styling within a single file.

Think of a SFC as a well-organized package containing everything a component needs: its visual structure (HTML), its behavior (JavaScript), and its look and feel (CSS). This makes it easier to reason about, maintain, and reuse your components.

What is a Single-File Component? - A Complete Package

A Single-File Component (SFC) is a .vue file that encapsulates a component's template, script, and style in a single file. It leverages specific tags to encapsulate the component's concerns.

A .vue file typically contains three top-level sections:

- **<template>:** Contains the component's HTML template. This is where you define the structure of your component's user interface using Vue.js template syntax.
- **<script>:** Contains the component's JavaScript logic. This is where you define your data properties, computed properties, methods, lifecycle hooks, and other JavaScript code. The script section must export a Vue component object.
- **<style>:** Contains the component's CSS styles. You can use scoped styles to limit the styles to a specific component, or you can use global styles that apply to the entire application. This section is optional.

An Example of a .vue File: The "Hello World" Edition

Here's a simple example of a .vue file:

```
<template>
  <div>
    <h1>{{ message }}</h1>
  </div>
</template>

<script>
export default {
  data() {
    return {
```

```
        message: 'Hello from the component!'
      };
    }
  };
</script>

<style scoped>
h1 {
  color: blue;
}
</style>
```

Dissecting the Code:

1. **<template>:** Contains the HTML template for the component. In this case, it's a simple div with an h1 tag that displays the message data property.
2. **<script>:** Contains the JavaScript logic for the component.
   - export default { ... }: This is the key to making the component reusable. The export default statement exports a Vue component object that can be imported and used in other components or in your main application.
   - data() { ... }: Defines the component's data properties. In this case, we have a single data property called message.
3. **<style scoped>:** Contains the CSS styles for the component.
   - scoped: The scoped attribute limits the styles to the current component. This prevents the styles from leaking out and affecting other parts of your application.

Benefits of Using Single-File Components: Why Make the Switch?

Switching to SFCs provides numerous advantages:

- **Improved Organization:** Keeps all related code in one place. It significantly simplifies reasoning about and maintaining components, especially as they grow more complex.
- **Enhanced Readability:** Syntax highlighting (with proper editor support) and clear separation of concerns make your code easier to read and understand.
- **CSS Scoping:** Prevents style collisions by limiting the scope of CSS styles to the component. This is crucial for building large applications with many components and preventing unexpected style conflicts.

- **Pre-processing Power:** Supports pre-processors like Sass, Less, and Stylus. This allows you to use advanced CSS features like variables, mixins, and nesting, making your styles more maintainable and efficient.
- **Build Tool Integration:** Works seamlessly with build tools like Vue CLI and Vite. These tools provide a development server, hot-reloading, and other features that significantly improve the development experience.

Setting Up Your Development Environment: The Tools You'll Need

To use Single-File Components, you'll need to set up a build process using a tool like Vue CLI or Vite. These tools will compile your .vue files into standard JavaScript, HTML and CSS that can be used in the browser.

Both Vue CLI and Vite are excellent choices, but Vite is generally faster and more lightweight.

1. Using Vue CLI (Command Line Interface):

If you don't have Vue CLI installed, install it globally:

```
npm install -g @vue/cli
# OR
yarn global add @vue/cli
```

Create a new Vue project:

```
vue create my-project
```

During the project creation process, you'll be prompted to choose a preset. Select the "Default (Vue 3 Preview)" preset or manually configure your project to include Babel and a CSS pre-processor if you want to use them.

2. Using Vite (Next Generation Frontend Tooling):

Vite is a build tool that aims to provide a faster and leaner development experience for modern web projects.

Create a new Vue project:

```
npm create vite@latest my-project --template vue
# OR
yarn create vite my-project --template vue
```

Install dependencies:

```
cd my-project
npm install
# OR
yarn install
```

Running Your Development Server:

Once you've set up your project, you can start the development server:

Vue CLI:

```
cd my-project
npm run serve
# OR
yarn serve
```

Vite:

```
cd my-project
npm run dev
# OR
yarn dev
```

This will start a development server that automatically reloads your application whenever you make changes to your code.

Importing and Using .vue Components: Putting it All Together

Now that you have a build process set up, you can import and use your .vue components in other components or in your main application:

```
<template>
  <div>
    <h1>My Parent Component</h1>
    <MyComponent message="Hello from the parent!"></MyComponent>
```

```
  </div>
</template>

<script>
import MyComponent from './MyComponent.vue'; // Import the
.vue file

export default {
  components: {
    MyComponent // Register the component
  }
};
</script>
```

In this example, we import the MyComponent from the MyComponent.vue file and register it in the components option of the parent component. We can then use the MyComponent in the parent component's template.

Personal Insight: My Shift to SFCs: The Turning Point

Switching to Single-File Components was a turning point in my Vue.js development. Before that, I was struggling to manage the complexity of my applications. SFCs provided the structure and organization I needed to build larger and more maintainable projects.

Conclusion: Embrace the SFC Revolution!

Single-File Components are a powerful and essential feature of Vue.js development. By using SFCs, you can create more organized, maintainable, and scalable applications. If you're not already using SFCs, I highly recommend that you make the switch today.

3.6 Dynamic Components – Rendering Components Based on Data: The Art of Adaptable UIs

In many applications, you need to render different components based on a specific condition or data property. Imagine creating a tabbed interface where the content of each tab is a separate component, or a form that dynamically renders different input fields based on user selections. Dynamic components enable precisely this sort of adaptable and flexible UI. They allow you to switch between components on the fly, creating a more interactive and responsive user experience.

Think of dynamic components as a chameleon that can change its appearance to blend in with its surroundings. The component tag, combined with the :is attribute, allows Vue to seamlessly swap one component for another, giving you immense control over the structure of your user interface.

The Key: The <component :is="..."> Tag

The heart of dynamic components lies in the <component :is="..."> tag. This special tag tells Vue to render a component based on the value of the :is attribute. The value of the :is attribute can be a component name (string) or a component object.

```
<component :is="currentComponent"></component>
```

Here, currentComponent is a data property in your Vue instance that determines which component will be rendered. If currentComponent is set to "component-a", Vue will render the component-a component. If it's set to "component-b", Vue will render the component-b component, and so on.

Step-by-Step Implementation: From Data to UI

Let's walk through a step-by-step example to illustrate how to implement dynamic components:

1. Define Your Components:

First, you need to define the components that you want to render dynamically. These can be any valid Vue components, including those defined in separate .vue files.

```
const ComponentA = {
  template: '<div>Component A Content</div>'
};

const ComponentB = {
  template: '<div>Component B Content</div>'
};
```

2. Register Your Components:

Register these components (either globally or locally) as before. For this example, we'll register them locally.

```
      const { createApp } = Vue;

const app = createApp({
  components: {
    ComponentA,
    ComponentB
  },
  data() {
    return {
      currentComponent: 'ComponentA' // Initial component
    };
  },
  template: `
    <div>
      <button @click="currentComponent = 'ComponentA'">Show
Component A</button>
      <button @click="currentComponent = 'ComponentB'">Show
Component B</button>
      <component :is="currentComponent"></component>
    </div>
  `
});

app.mount('#app');
```

3. Use the <component :is="..."> Tag:

In the template of the parent component, use the <component :is="..."> tag to render the dynamic component. Bind the :is attribute to a data property that determines which component to render.

4. Control the Data Property:

Modify the data property that you bound to the :is attribute to switch between components. In our example, we use buttons to change the currentComponent data property, triggering Vue to re-render the <component> tag with the new component.

Explanation:

- We defined two simple components, ComponentA and ComponentB.

- We registered them locally in the parent component's components option.
- We added a currentComponent data property to store the name of the component to render.
- We used the <component :is="..."> tag to render the dynamic component, binding the :is attribute to the currentComponent data property.
- We added buttons that update the currentComponent data property, causing Vue to switch between ComponentA and ComponentB.

The Power of Component Objects: A More Flexible Approach

Instead of binding the :is attribute to a component *name*, you can bind it to a component *object*. This can be useful in situations where you need to dynamically create or modify components at runtime.

```
        const { createApp } = Vue;

const app = createApp({
  components: {
    ComponentA: {
      template: '<div>Component A Content (with dynamic
prop): {{ dynamicProp }}</div>',
      props: ['dynamicProp']
    }
  },
  data() {
    return {
      showComponentA: true,
      dynamicPropValue: "Initial Value"
    };
  },
  computed: {
    currentComponent() {
      return this.showComponentA ? ComponentA : null; // Or
another component object
    }
  },
  template: `
    <div>
      <button @click="showComponentA =
!showComponentA">Toggle Component A</button>
      <component :is="currentComponent" :dynamic-
prop="dynamicPropValue"></component>
    </div>
  `
});
```

```
app.mount('#app');
```

Explanation:

- We toggle showComponentA to conditionally return the ComponentA component object in our currentComponent computed property.
- We set ComponentA to null if showComponentA is false. You can use another component if you want, too.
- We passed dynamicPropValue to the dynamic component.

This example shows how you can combine conditional logic with dynamic components to create even more flexible user interfaces.

Key Considerations:

- **Lifecycle Hooks:** When switching between dynamic components, Vue will properly unmount the previous component and mount the new component, triggering the appropriate lifecycle hooks (e.g., mounted, unmounted).
- **Keeping State Alive:** By default, Vue will destroy the state of the old component when switching to a new one. If you want to preserve the state of the old component, you can use the <keep-alive> component.
- **Performance:** While dynamic components are powerful, they can also have a performance impact if you switch between them frequently. If you experience performance issues, consider optimizing your components or using a different approach.

The <keep-alive> Component: Preserving State

The <keep-alive> component allows you to preserve the state of dynamic components when switching between them. This can be useful for improving the user experience by preventing components from being re-rendered every time they are activated.

```
    <keep-alive>
  <component :is="currentComponent"></component>
</keep-alive>
```

When you wrap a dynamic component with <keep-alive>, Vue will cache the component's state and reuse it when the component is re-activated.

Practical Example: A Tabbed Interface

Let's create a practical example of a tabbed interface that uses dynamic components to render the content of each tab:

```
<!DOCTYPE html>
<html>
<head>
  <title>Tabbed Interface</title>
  <script
src="https://unpkg.com/vue@3/dist/vue.global.js"></script>
  <style>
    .tab-button {
      padding: 10px 20px;
      border: 1px solid #ccc;
      background-color: #f0f0f0;
      cursor: pointer;
    }
    .tab-button.active {
      background-color: #ddd;
    }
  </style>
</head>
<body>
  <div id="app">
    <div class="tabs">
      <button
        class="tab-button"
        :class="{ active: currentTab === 'HomeTab' }"
        @click="currentTab = 'HomeTab'"
      >Home</button>
      <button
        class="tab-button"
        :class="{ active: currentTab === 'AboutTab' }"
        @click="currentTab = 'AboutTab'"
      >About</button>
      <button
        class="tab-button"
        :class="{ active: currentTab === 'ContactTab' }"
        @click="currentTab = 'ContactTab'"
      >Contact</button>
    </div>

    <component :is="currentTabComponent"></component>
  </div>
```

```
  <script>
    const { createApp, computed } = Vue;

    const HomeTab = {
      template: '<div><h2>Home</h2><p>Welcome to the home
page!</p></div>'
    };

    const AboutTab = {
      template: '<div><h2>About</h2><p>Learn more about
us.</p></div>'
    };

    const ContactTab = {
      template: '<div><h2>Contact</h2><p>Get in touch with
us.</p></div>'
    };

    const app = createApp({
      data() {
        return {
          currentTab: 'HomeTab'
        };
      },
      computed: {
        currentTabComponent() {
          return this.currentTab === 'HomeTab'
            ? HomeTab
            : this.currentTab === 'AboutTab'
              ? AboutTab
              : ContactTab;
        }
      },
      components: {
        HomeTab,
        AboutTab,
        ContactTab
      }
    });

    app.mount('#app');
  </script>
</body>
</html>
```

Explanation:

1. **Tab Components:** We define three components: HomeTab, AboutTab, and ContactTab.

2. **currentTab Data Property:** The currentTab data property stores the name of the currently selected tab.
3. **currentTabComponent Computed Property:** The currentTabComponent computed property returns the component object that corresponds to the currentTab value.
4. **<component :is="...">:** The <component :is="currentTabComponent"></component> tag renders the dynamic component based on the value of the currentTabComponent computed property.
5. **Tab Buttons:** The tab buttons update the currentTab data property when clicked, causing Vue to switch between the tab components.

Personal Insight: Dynamic Components Unleash Creativity

Dynamic components are like a superpower for UI development. They enable you to create user interfaces that are highly adaptable and responsive to user interactions.

Conclusion: Mastering Adaptable UIs

Dynamic components are an essential tool for building flexible and dynamic Vue.js applications. By understanding how to use the <component :is="..."> tag, how to manage component state, and how to use <keep-alive>, you can create user interfaces that are both powerful and user-friendly. This completes our journey into Components.

Part 2: The Reactivity System and Composition API

Chapter 4: Understanding Vue's Reactivity – The Magic Behind the Scenes

Welcome to the core of Vue.js: the reactivity system! Up until now, we've *used* reactivity, but now we're going to pull back the curtain and see *how* it works. Understanding reactivity is crucial for writing efficient, predictable, and maintainable Vue.js applications. It's what allows Vue to automatically update the DOM whenever your data changes, making it feel like your UI is magically in sync with your application's state.

Think of Vue's reactivity system as a meticulously designed network of sensors and triggers. When your data changes, the sensors detect the change and trigger a chain of updates that automatically update the parts of your user interface that depend on that data. Without this system, you'd have to manually update the DOM every time your data changes, which would be tedious and error-prone.

4.1 How Reactivity Works – The Inner Workings Unveiled: Demystifying the Magic

Vue.js is renowned for its reactive nature. It's the magic behind how data changes automatically reflect in the user interface, minimizing manual DOM manipulation. But how does this reactivity *actually* work? In this section, we'll take a deep dive into the inner workings of Vue's reactivity system, unraveling its core mechanisms and revealing the techniques it employs to achieve its seemingly effortless data synchronization.

The Pre-Vue 3 World: Object.defineProperty (A Historical Note)

In Vue 2, the reactivity system relied heavily on JavaScript's Object.defineProperty. This method allows you to define and modify the properties of an object, including intercepting property access and modification attempts. Vue 2 used Object.defineProperty to wrap each data property, adding getters and setters that tracked dependencies and triggered updates.

However, Object.defineProperty has some limitations:

- **Deep Reactivity Required Traversal:** Reactivity needed to deeply traverse the object tree to convert every property.

- **Cannot Detect Property Addition/Deletion:** Object.defineProperty is unable to detect property additions or deletions. Adding and deleting properties could not be tracked for rendering updates.
- **Limited to Objects:** It only works with object properties, not with entire objects or arrays.

While understanding the Object.defineProperty approach offers valuable context, Vue 3 has evolved to use a more efficient system.

Vue 3 and Beyond: The Proxy Revolution (and Reflect, its Sidekick)

Vue 3 and later versions adopt JavaScript's built-in Proxy object. Proxy provides more powerful interception capabilities, addressing the limitations of Object.defineProperty and enabling a more performant and flexible reactivity system.

What is a Proxy Object?

A Proxy object is a wrapper around another object (the *target* object) that intercepts operations on that object. It allows you to define custom behavior for fundamental operations like getting, setting, deleting properties, and even calling functions.

Key Advantages of Using Proxy:

- **Dynamic Interception:** Proxy can intercept any operation on the target object, including property access, modification, and deletion.
- **No Deep Traversal Required Initially:** Proxies do not require the framework to traverse deeply into the object's nested properties upon creation. Properties are made reactive only when accessed, leading to significant performance improvements, especially with deeply nested object structures.
- **Support for New Properties:** Proxy can detect the addition of new properties to the target object.
- **Support for Deletion:** Proxy can detect the deletion of properties from the target object.

The Role of Reflect: A Partner in Crime

Along with Proxy, Vue 3 also leverages JavaScript's Reflect object. Reflect provides a set of static methods that mirror the built-in operators and functions of JavaScript. By using Reflect in conjunction with Proxy, Vue.js can ensure that the intercepted operations behave as expected, while still allowing the framework to track dependencies and trigger updates.

A Concrete Example: The Proxy in Action

Let's illustrate how Proxy works with a simplified example:

```
      //The Observer instance that will watch the values
change
class Observer {
  constructor(cb) {
    this.cb = cb
  }

  update() {
    this.cb()
  }
}

//The Dependency instance that will hold a list of
subscribers
class Dependency {
  constructor() {
    this.observers = []
  }

  subscribe(observer) {
    this.observers.push(observer)
  }

  notify() {
    this.observers.forEach(observer => {
      observer.update()
    })
  }
}

//The Vue Instance
class VueInstance {
  constructor(options) {
    this._data = options.data()
    this.observer = null
    this.proxy = null

    this.createProxy()
  }

  createProxy() {
    let dep = new Dependency()
    let vm = this
```

```
    let proxy = new Proxy(this._data, {
      get(target, key) {
        console.log(`GETTING ${key}`)

        return Reflect.get(target, key)
      },
      set(target, key, value) {
        console.log(`SETTING ${key} to ${value}`)

        let result = Reflect.set(target, key, value)

        if (result) {
          dep.notify()
        }

        return result
      }
    })

    this.observer = new Observer(() => {
      console.log("Value updated in view")
    })

    dep.subscribe(this.observer)
    this.proxy = proxy
  }
}

let vm = new VueInstance({
  data() {
    return {
      name: "John",
      age: 20
    }
  }
})

console.log(vm.proxy.age)
vm.proxy.age = 30
```

Explanation:

1. We create a new Proxy object, wrapping our data object.
2. In the get trap, we log the property being accessed using Reflect.get.
3. In the set trap, we log the property being set and its new value using Reflect.set.

4. Whenever a property is set a notify is triggered, calling every subscriber.

This code represents a simplified version of Vue's reactivity system. Here's an explanation of what the code does:

- **Observer Class**: Represents a subscriber that reacts to data changes by executing a callback function (cb). It has an update method that's triggered when notified of a change.
- **Dependency Class**: Manages a list of observers (subscribers) and notifies them when a data change occurs. It has methods to subscribe (add) observers and notify (trigger) all observers to update.
- **VueInstance Class**: Represents the Vue instance and sets up reactivity for the provided data.
    - **constructor(options)**: Initializes the instance with the data provided in options.data(). It creates a Proxy for the data, which intercepts property accesses and modifications.
    - **createProxy()**: Sets up the Proxy to intercept property accesses (get) and modifications (set). The Proxy's set method includes logic to notify all subscribers (observers) of the data change.
    - **Proxy get method**: Logs a message to the console when a property is accessed
    - **Proxy set method**: Logs a message to the console when a property is modified and then notifies all subscribers that the value has changed
- **Usage**:
    - A VueInstance is created with some initial data (name and age).
    - The proxy object logs the access of age, sets the age to 30, and then logs the updated value.

The Reactivity Flow (Simplified):

1. **Create Reactive Data:** Use reactive() or ref() to create reactive data.
2. **Vue Creates Proxy:** Vue wraps your data with a Proxy object.
3. **Component Accesses Data:** When a component accesses a reactive data property, the Proxy object tracks the dependency.
4. **Data is Modified:** When you modify the data, the Proxy intercepts the change.
5. **Proxy Notifies Components:** The Proxy notifies all components that depend on the changed data.

6. **Components Re-render:** The components re-render, updating the DOM.

Personal Insight: The Elegance of Proxies

The transition from Object.defineProperty to Proxy was a significant improvement in Vue's architecture. The increased flexibility and efficiency of Proxy allowed the Vue team to build a more powerful and maintainable reactivity system.

Conclusion: Unveiling the Magic

By understanding the inner workings of Vue's reactivity system, you can write more efficient, predictable, and maintainable Vue.js applications. You'll have a deeper appreciation for how Vue.js automatically updates the DOM whenever your data changes, freeing you from the tedious task of manual DOM manipulation. In the next section, we'll explore ref and reactive, the main API's that can help you build your own Vue reactive system.

4.2 Reactive Primitives: ref and reactive – The Building Blocks of Reactivity: Choosing the Right Tool for the Job

Now that we've demystified *how* Vue's reactivity system works, let's explore the two fundamental tools it provides for *creating* reactive data: ref and reactive. These are the foundational APIs you'll use daily to make your data "come alive" and automatically update your user interfaces. Understanding the nuances of each and when to use them is key to effective Vue.js development.

Think of ref and reactive as different types of containers for your data. ref is designed for holding single, primitive values, while reactive is designed for holding complex objects and arrays. Choosing the right container for your data will ensure that Vue's reactivity system can track changes efficiently and effectively.

Importing the Essentials: Getting Started

Before you can use ref and reactive, you need to import them from the vue module:

```
import { ref, reactive } from 'vue';
```

ref: Creating Reactive References to Primitive Values

The ref function is used to create reactive references to single, primitive values like numbers, strings, booleans, and even null or undefined. It takes an initial value as its argument and returns a *ref object*. This ref object has a single property called .value that holds the actual value.

```
const count = ref(0); // Create a reactive reference to a number
const message = ref('Hello!'); // Create a reactive reference to a string
const isLoggedIn = ref(false); // Create a reactive reference to a boolean
```

To access or modify the value of a ref, you *must* use the .value property:

```
console.log(count.value); // Output: 0

count.value++; // Increment the count

console.log(count.value); // Output: 1

message.value = 'Goodbye!'; // Update the message

console.log(message.value); // Output: Goodbye!
```

But There's an Exception: Template Unwrapping

Inside your component's template, you *don't* need to use the .value property to access ref values. Vue.js automatically unwraps refs in templates, making them easier to use.

```
<template>
  <div>
    <p>Count: {{ count }}</p> <button
@click="count++">Increment</button>
    <p>Message: {{ message }}</p>
  </div>
</template>

<script>
```

```
import { ref } from 'vue';

export default {
  setup() {
    const count = ref(0);
    const message = ref('Hello!');

    return {
      count,
      message
    };
  }
};
</script>
```

Why the .value Property? (and why it's not needed in templates)

The .value property is necessary because ref is designed to hold a *reference* to a value, not the value itself. This allows Vue.js to track changes to the value even when it's being passed around to different parts of your application.

The automatic unwrapping in templates is a convenience feature that makes your templates cleaner and more readable.

reactive: Creating Reactive Objects and Arrays

The reactive function is used to create reactive objects and arrays. It takes an object or an array as its argument and returns a reactive proxy of that object or array. All the properties of the object or array are made reactive, meaning that any changes to those properties will trigger updates in the DOM.

```
      const state = reactive({
  name: 'John Doe',
  age: 30
});

const items = reactive(['Apple', 'Banana', 'Orange']);
```

To access or modify the properties of a reactive object, you use the standard dot notation or bracket notation:

```
      console.log(state.name); // Output: John Doe
```

```
state.age = 31; // Update the age

console.log(state.age); // Output: 31

items.push('Grape'); // Add an item to the array

console.log(items); // Output: ['Apple', 'Banana', 'Orange',
'Grape']
```

Key Considerations for reactive:

1. **Primitives Must Be Wrapped:** You can't pass primitive values directly to reactive. If you need to make a primitive value reactive, wrap it in an object:

```
const state = reactive({
  count: 0 // Correct: count is a property of an object
});
```

2. **No Complete Object Replacement:** Replacing a reactive object with a completely new object will break the reactivity. You should only modify the *properties* of the reactive object, not the object itself. If you need to replace the entire object, use ref instead.
3. **Shallow Reactivity By Default:** reactive is *shallowly* reactive. It makes the top-level properties of the object reactive, but it doesn't automatically make nested objects or arrays reactive. To make nested properties reactive, you need to use reactive recursively, or use deepRef() (explained later).

toRefs: Maintaining Reactivity While Destructuring Objects

One common pitfall with reactive is that destructuring it breaks the reactivity. If you destructure a reactive object, the destructured variables will become plain JavaScript values, and changes to those variables will *not* trigger updates in the DOM.

To avoid this problem, you can use the toRefs function. toRefs converts each property of a reactive object into a ref, allowing you to destructure the object while maintaining reactivity:

```
import { reactive, toRefs } from 'vue';

const state = reactive({
```

```
  name: 'John Doe',
  age: 30
});

const { name, age } = toRefs(state); // Convert to refs

console.log(name.value); // Output: John Doe
console.log(age.value); // Output: 30

name.value = 'Jane Doe'; // This will update state.name
age.value = 31; // This will update state.age
```

Choosing Between ref and reactive: A Guiding Principle

Here's a simple guiding principle for choosing between ref and reactive:

- **ref:** Use ref for single, primitive values (numbers, strings, booleans) and when you need to completely replace an object or array.
- **reactive:** Use reactive for complex objects and arrays that you want to modify in place.

A Practical Example: Managing a User Profile

Let's create a practical example of managing a user profile using ref and reactive:

```
    <!DOCTYPE html>
<html>
<head>
  <title>User Profile</title>
  <script
src="https://unpkg.com/vue@3/dist/vue.global.js"></script>
</head>
<body>
  <div id="app">
    <h2>User Profile</h2>
    <p>Name: {{ name }}</p>
    <p>Age: {{ age }}</p>
    <p>Is Active: {{ profile.isActive }}</p>

    <button @click="updateName">Update Name</button>
    <button @click="profile.isActive =
!profile.isActive">Toggle Active</button>
  </div>

  <script>
    const { createApp, ref, reactive } = Vue;
```

```
    const app = createApp({
      setup() {
        const name = ref('John Doe');
        const age = ref(30);
        const profile = reactive({
          isActive: true
        });

        const updateName = () => {
          name.value = 'Jane Doe';
        };

        return {
          name,
          age,
          profile,
          updateName
        };
      }
    });

    app.mount('#app');
  </script>
</body>
</html>
```

Explanation:

- We use ref for the name and age properties, as they are simple primitive values.
- We use reactive for the profile object, as it's a complex object with multiple properties.
- We can directly modify the isActive property of the profile object, and the DOM will be updated automatically.
- We can update the name value using the updateName method, which sets the .value property of the name ref.

Personal Insight: The Aha! Moment with refs

I remember being initially confused by the need to use .value with refs. It seemed like an unnecessary complication. But once I understood the underlying mechanism of how refs work, it made perfect sense. The .value property is what allows Vue to track changes to the value and trigger updates in the DOM.

Conclusion: Mastering the Building Blocks

ref and reactive are the foundational building blocks of Vue's reactivity system. By understanding how to use them effectively, you can create dynamic and responsive Vue.js applications. In the next section, we'll explore Computed Properties.

4.3 Computed Properties: Deriving Data – Smart and Efficient: Let the Framework Do the Work

As you build more complex Vue.js applications, you'll often find yourself needing to derive new data from existing data. This is where computed properties come in. Computed properties are properties that are dynamically calculated based on other reactive data properties in your component. They are a powerful and efficient way to keep your data consistent and up-to-date.

Think of computed properties as intelligent, self-updating variables. Instead of manually recalculating a value whenever its dependencies change, you define a computed property, and Vue takes care of the rest. It automatically tracks the dependencies of the computed property and re-evaluates it only when those dependencies change.

Why Computed Properties? The Benefits Unveiled

Computed properties offer several key benefits over simply using methods in your templates:

- **Caching:** Computed properties are cached based on their dependencies. This means that they are only re-evaluated when their dependencies change. This can significantly improve performance, especially for expensive calculations.
- **Dependency Tracking:** Vue automatically tracks the dependencies of computed properties. This means that Vue knows exactly when to re-evaluate the computed property. You don't have to manually tell Vue which data properties the computed property depends on.
- **Readability:** Computed properties make your code more readable and maintainable by clearly expressing how data is derived from other data.
- **Simplicity:** Templates stay simpler and cleaner.

Defining Computed Properties: Two Approaches

Vue offers two primary syntaxes for defining computed properties:

1. Getter-Only (The Most Common):

This is the most common and straightforward approach. You define a getter function that returns the value of the computed property.

```
      import { ref, computed } from 'vue';

const firstName = ref('John');
const lastName = ref('Doe');

const fullName = computed(() => {
  return firstName.value + ' ' + lastName.value;
});

console.log(fullName.value); // Output: John Doe

firstName.value = 'Jane';

console.log(fullName.value); // Output: Jane Doe
```

In this example, fullName is a computed property that returns the concatenation of firstName and lastName. Vue automatically tracks that fullName depends on firstName and lastName, and it will re-evaluate fullName whenever either of those values changes.

2. Getter and Setter (For Two-Way Data Binding):

This approach allows you to define both a getter and a setter function for the computed property. This is useful when you want to allow users to modify the computed property directly, and have those changes reflected in the underlying data properties. This is less common, but important to know.

```
      import { ref, computed } from 'vue';

const firstName = ref('John');
const lastName = ref('Doe');

const fullName = computed({
  get: () => {
    return firstName.value + ' ' + lastName.value;
  },
  set: (newValue) => {
    const [newFirstName, newLastName] = newValue.split(' ');
    firstName.value = newFirstName;
```

```
    lastName.value = newLastName;
  }
});

console.log(fullName.value); // Output: John Doe

fullName.value = 'Jane Smith'; // Update fullName

console.log(firstName.value); // Output: Jane
console.log(lastName.value); // Output: Smith
```

In this example, fullName has both a getter and a setter. The getter returns the concatenation of firstName and lastName, as before. The setter splits the new value into two parts and updates firstName and lastName accordingly. This allows you to modify fullName directly, and have those changes reflected in the underlying data properties.

Important Considerations:

- **Keep Getters Pure:** The getter function of a computed property should be pure, meaning that it should not have any side effects. It should only return a value based on its dependencies, and it should not modify any external state.
- **Handle Setters Carefully:** The setter function of a computed property should be used to update the underlying data properties in a consistent and predictable way. Avoid complex logic or side effects in the setter.
- **Avoid Circular Dependencies:** Be careful to avoid creating circular dependencies between computed properties. This can lead to infinite loops and performance issues.

The Power of Caching: Efficiency in Action

To illustrate the benefits of caching, let's consider an example with a computationally expensive calculation:

```
      import { ref, computed } from 'vue';

const count = ref(0);

const expensiveCalculation = () => {
  console.log('Performing expensive calculation...');
  // Simulate a time-consuming operation
  let result = 0;
```

```
  for (let i = 0; i < 100000000; i++) {
    result += i;
  }
  return result;
};

const computedResult = computed(() => {
  return expensiveCalculation() + count.value;
});

console.log(computedResult.value); // Expensive calculation
is performed
console.log(computedResult.value); // Result is retrieved
from cache

count.value++;

console.log(computedResult.value); // Expensive calculation
is performed again
console.log(computedResult.value); // Result is retrieved
from cache
```

In this example, the expensiveCalculation function simulates a time-consuming operation. The computedResult computed property depends on the result of this calculation and the count data property.

The first time you access computedResult.value, the expensiveCalculation function is called, and the result is stored in the cache. Subsequent accesses to computedResult.value will retrieve the result from the cache, without re-executing the expensiveCalculation function.

When you increment the count data property, Vue detects that the computedResult depends on count, and it re-evaluates the computed property. This triggers the expensiveCalculation function to be called again, and the new result is stored in the cache.

This caching mechanism can significantly improve the performance of your application, especially for computed properties that involve complex calculations or data transformations.

Practical Example: A Shopping Cart Total

Let's create a practical example of calculating a shopping cart total using computed properties:

```
    <!DOCTYPE html>
<html>
<head>
  <title>Shopping Cart</title>
  <script
src="https://unpkg.com/vue@3/dist/vue.global.js"></script>
</head>
<body>
  <div id="app">
    <h2>Shopping Cart</h2>
    <ul>
      <li v-for="item in cart" :key="item.id">
        {{ item.name }} - ${{ item.price }} - Quantity: {{
item.quantity }}
      </li>
    </ul>
    <h3>Total: ${{ cartTotal }}</h3>
  </div>

  <script>
    const { createApp, ref, computed } = Vue;

    const app = createApp({
      setup() {
        const cart = ref([
          { id: 1, name: 'Product A', price: 10, quantity: 2
},
          { id: 2, name: 'Product B', price: 20, quantity: 1
}
        ]);

        const cartTotal = computed(() => {
          return cart.value.reduce((total, item) => {
            return total + item.price * item.quantity;
          }, 0);
        });

        return {
          cart,
          cartTotal
        };
      }
    });

    app.mount('#app');
  </script>
</body>
</html>
```

In this example, the cartTotal computed property calculates the total value of all items in the cart array. Vue automatically tracks that cartTotal depends on the cart array, and it will re-evaluate cartTotal whenever the cart array changes.

Personal Insight: Computed Properties: A Code Clarity Boost

I've found that using computed properties not only improves performance but also significantly enhances code readability. By moving complex calculations out of my templates and into computed properties, I make my templates much cleaner and easier to understand.

Conclusion: The Power of Smart Data

Computed properties are a powerful tool for deriving data in Vue.js applications. By understanding how to define computed properties, how they are cached, and when to use them, you can create more efficient, maintainable, and readable code. With this you can use the power of Vue to perform any type of calculation. In the next section, we'll explore Watchers.

4.4 Watchers: Responding to Changes – The Reactive Observers: Taking Action When Data Evolves

While computed properties excel at *deriving* data, *watchers* provide a mechanism to execute side effects in response to data changes. A "side effect" is any operation that interacts with the outside world, such as making an API call, updating a local storage value, or logging a message to the console. Watchers act as observers, vigilantly monitoring specific data properties and triggering a callback function whenever those properties change.

Think of watchers as reactive sentinels, always alert for changes in the data landscape and ready to execute a predefined set of actions when those changes occur. They allow you to build applications that react dynamically to user input, server updates, or any other event that modifies your data.

Defining Watchers: Two Powerful Approaches

Vue.js offers two primary ways to define watchers:

1. **The watch Function: Precise Control and Granularity**

The watch function provides the most granular control over how you respond to data changes. It takes two essential arguments:

- **The Source:** This specifies the data property or expression you want to watch. This can be a ref, a reactive property, a getter function, or even an array of data sources.
- **The Callback:** This function is executed whenever the source data changes. It receives the new value and the old value of the source as arguments.

```
import { ref, watch } from 'vue';

const inputValue = ref('');

watch(
  inputValue,
  (newValue, oldValue) => {
    console.log(`inputValue changed from ${oldValue} to
${newValue}`);
    // Perform a side effect, like making an API call
  }
);

inputValue.value = 'Hello'; // Output: inputValue changed
from  to Hello
```

In this example, we're watching the inputValue ref. Whenever its value changes, the callback function logs a message to the console.

Watching Multiple Sources:

You can also watch multiple data sources at once by passing an array to the watch function:

```
import { ref, watch } from 'vue';

const firstName = ref('John');
const lastName = ref('Doe');

watch(
  [firstName, lastName],
  ([newFirstName, newLastName], [oldFirstName, oldLastName])
=> {
    console.log(`Name changed from ${oldFirstName}
${oldLastName} to ${newFirstName} ${newLastName}`);
  }
```

```
);

firstName.value = 'Jane'; // Output: Name changed from John
Doe to Jane Doe
```

Options for Advanced Control:

The watch function also accepts an optional third argument: an object that allows you to configure the watcher's behavior:

- **immediate: true:** This option causes the callback function to be executed immediately when the watcher is created, before any data changes have occurred.
- **deep: true:** This option enables deep watching. When deep is set to true, the watcher will also track changes to nested properties within objects and arrays.

```
import { reactive, watch } from 'vue';

const state = reactive({
  user: {
    name: 'John Doe',
    age: 30
  }
});

watch(
  () => state.user,
  (newValue, oldValue) => {
    console.log('User object changed');
  },
  { deep: true }
);

state.user.name = 'Jane Doe'; // Output: User object changed
```

- **flush: 'pre' | 'post' | 'sync':** This option controls when the watcher callback is executed relative to the component's render cycle. pre (default) runs the callback before the DOM is updated, post runs it after the DOM is updated, and sync runs it immediately after the data change (not recommended for performance reasons).

- **onTrack and onTrigger:** These options allow you to debug the watcher's dependency tracking by providing callbacks that are executed when dependencies are tracked or triggered.

1. **The watchEffect Function: Streamlined Side Effects**

The watchEffect function provides a more streamlined way to perform side effects that depend on reactive data. It automatically tracks all the reactive dependencies used within its callback function, eliminating the need to explicitly specify which data properties to watch.

```
      import { ref, watchEffect } from 'vue';

const count = ref(0);
const doubled = ref(0);

watchEffect(() => {
  doubled.value = count.value * 2; // Automatically tracks
'count'
  console.log(`Doubled value updated to ${doubled.value}`);
});

count.value++; // 'doubled' is automatically updated
```

In this example, watchEffect automatically detects that the callback function depends on the count ref, so it will re-run the callback whenever count changes.

Key Differences Between watch and watchEffect:

- **Dependency Tracking:** watch requires you to explicitly specify the data properties to watch, while watchEffect automatically tracks dependencies.
- **Callback Execution:** watch's callback is only executed when the specified data properties change, while watchEffect's callback is executed initially and whenever any of its dependencies change.
- **Old Value Access:** watch provides access to both the new value and the old value of the data property, while watchEffect only provides access to the new value.

When to Use watch vs. watchEffect:

- **watch:** Use watch when you need precise control over which data properties to watch, when you need access to both the old and new values, and when you want to perform a specific action only when certain data properties change.
- **watchEffect:** Use watchEffect when you have a simple side effect that depends on several reactive data properties and you don't need access to the old values.

Practical Example: Debouncing an API Call

Let's create a practical example of debouncing an API call using watchers:

```
<!DOCTYPE html>
<html>
<head>
  <title>Debounced API Call</title>
  <script
src="https://unpkg.com/vue@3/dist/vue.global.js"></script>
</head>
<body>
  <div id="app">
    <input type="text" v-model="searchTerm"
placeholder="Search...">
  </div>

  <script>
    const { createApp, ref, watch } = Vue;

    const app = createApp({
      setup() {
        const searchTerm = ref('');

        const searchApi = async (term) => {
          console.log(`Calling API with search term:
${term}`);
          // Simulate an API call
          return new Promise(resolve => {
            setTimeout(() => {
              resolve(`Results for: ${term}`);
            }, 500);
          });
        };

        const debouncedSearch = debounce(async (term) => {
          const results = await searchApi(term);
          console.log(results);
        }, 500); // Debounce for 500ms
```

```
        watch(
          searchTerm,
          (newValue) => {
            debouncedSearch(newValue);
          }
        );

        function debounce(func, delay) {
          let timeoutId;
          return function(...args) {
            clearTimeout(timeoutId);
            timeoutId = setTimeout(() => {
              func.apply(this, args);
            }, delay);
          };
        }

        return {
          searchTerm
        };
      }
    });

    app.mount('#app');
  </script>
</body>
</html>
```

Explanation:

1. We import Vue's functionalities and define a debouncing function.
2. We create a searchTerm ref bound to the input.
3. We use watch to monitor the searchTerm. When it changes, we call debouncedSearch. This ensures that the API call is only made after the user has stopped typing for a specified period.

Personal Insight: Watchers - The Key to Side Effect Control

Watchers have been invaluable for managing side effects in my Vue.js applications. They provide a clear and concise way to respond to data changes, ensuring that my application remains responsive and predictable.

Conclusion: Mastering Reactive Observation

Watchers and watchEffect are vital tools for responding to changes in your Vue.js applications. By understanding how they work, how to define them effectively, and when to use them, you can build more dynamic, responsive, and maintainable applications. In the next section, we'll learn about "Deep vs. Shallow Reactivity," giving you an important perspective on how to choose the best types of reactivity for your use case.

4.5 Deep vs. Shallow Reactivity – Understanding the Scope: Knowing How Deep the Rabbit Hole Goes

As you work with increasingly complex data structures in your Vue.js applications, it becomes crucial to understand the difference between deep and shallow reactivity. This distinction determines how Vue.js tracks changes within your data and triggers updates in the DOM. Choosing the appropriate type of reactivity can significantly impact the performance and behavior of your application.

Imagine you have a multi-level directory file system, where your main folder has subfolders with multiple files. Now imagine Vue's reactivity system tracking each file. The "deep vs shallow" determines if it just watches changes to the first main folder, or if it looks inside each subfolder too.

Understanding the Concepts:

- **Shallow Reactivity:** Only makes the direct properties of an object reactive. If those properties are themselves objects or arrays, changes within those nested structures will *not* be automatically detected by Vue.
- **Deep Reactivity:** Makes all properties of an object, including nested objects and arrays, reactive. Changes at any level of the data structure will trigger updates.

The Default: Shallow Reactivity with reactive

By default, the reactive function in Vue.js 3 creates a *shallowly* reactive object. This means that it only converts the immediate properties of the object into reactive properties. If any of those properties are themselves objects or arrays, changes within those nested structures will not be automatically detected by Vue's reactivity system.

```
    import { reactive } from 'vue';

const state = reactive({
  user: {
```

```
    name: 'John Doe',
    address: {
      street: '123 Main St',
      city: 'Anytown'
    }
  }
});

// Changing user.name will trigger an update
state.user.name = 'Jane Doe'; // This will trigger a DOM
update

// Changing state.user won't trigger updates on children
state.user = { name: 'Bob', address: { street: '456 Elm',
city: 'Otherville' } }; // Reassigning doesn't work

// Changing a nested address property directly will NOT
trigger an update because the address object wasn't reactive.
state.user.address.street = '789 Oak Ave'; // This will NOT
trigger a DOM update!! This is the pitfall!
```

Why Shallow Reactivity? (Performance Considerations)

Shallow reactivity is the default because it's more efficient. Deeply traversing and making every nested property reactive can be expensive, especially for large and complex data structures. By default, Vue only makes the direct properties reactive, which provides a good balance between reactivity and performance.

Creating Deep Reactivity: Two Common Approaches

If you need to make nested properties reactive, you have a few options:

1. Manual Application of reactive (Not Recommended for Deeply Nested Structures):

You can recursively apply the reactive function to each nested object or array. However, this approach can be tedious and error-prone, especially for deeply nested data structures.

```
      import { reactive } from 'vue';

const state = reactive({
  user: reactive({ //Make user object reactive
    name: 'John Doe',
    address: reactive({ //Make address object reactive
```

```
      street: '123 Main St',
      city: 'Anytown'
    })
  })
});
```

This makes setting properties such as state.user.address.street reactive, however there are other methods that are easier to maintain as your projects scale.

2. deepRef: Reactive all the way down (Most Common Solution):
Create a ref, then use Vue's markRaw to prevent reactivity on the deep levels of the object.

```
      import { ref, reactive, markRaw } from 'vue';

const state = ref({
  user: {
    name: 'John Doe',
    address: {
      street: '123 Main St',
      city: 'Anytown'
    }
  }
});

state.value.user = reactive(state.value.user); //Make user
object reactive
state.value.user.address =
reactive(state.value.user.address); //Make address object
reactive

console.log(state.value.user.name); //Access works
state.value.user.name = 'Bob'; //Change works

console.log(state.value.user.address.street) //Access works
state.value.user.address.street = 'Bob'; //Change works
```

While effective, this quickly becomes tedious for deeply nested properties.

Pitfalls to Avoid:

- **Reassigning Reactive Objects:** As mentioned earlier, replacing a reactive object with a completely new object will break the reactivity.

You should only modify the *properties* of the reactive object, not the object itself.

- **Mixing ref and reactive Incorrectly:** Don't try to use reactive on a ref's .value. They are designed for different purposes.

Practical Example: Managing a Nested Configuration Object

Let's create a practical example of managing a nested configuration object with deep reactivity:

```
<!DOCTYPE html>
<html>
<head>
  <title>Nested Configuration</title>
  <script
src="https://unpkg.com/vue@3/dist/vue.global.js"></script>
</head>
<body>
  <div id="app">
    <h2>Configuration</h2>
    <p>Theme: {{ config.theme.name }}</p>
    <p>Font Size: {{ config.theme.fontSize }}</p>
    <p>API URL: {{ config.api.url }}</p>

    <button @click="config.theme.name = 'Dark'">Change
Theme</button>
    <button @click="config.theme.fontSize = '18px'">Change
Font Size</button>
    <button @click="config.api.url =
'https://newapi.example.com'">Change API URL</button>
  </div>

  <script>
    const { createApp, reactive } = Vue;

    const app = createApp({
      setup() {
        const config = reactive({
          theme: {
            name: 'Light',
            fontSize: '16px'
          },
          api: {
            url: 'https://api.example.com'
          }
        });

        return {
          config
```

```
        };
      }
    });

    app.mount('#app');
  </script>
</body>
</html>
```

In this example, we have a config object with nested theme and api objects. The reactive function makes all properties of the config object, including the nested properties, reactive. This means that changes to any of the properties, such as config.theme.name or config.api.url, will trigger updates in the DOM.

Personal Insight: The Art of Balancing Performance and Reactivity

Choosing between deep and shallow reactivity is a matter of balancing performance and functionality. If you have a large and complex data structure, deep reactivity can be expensive. However, if you need to track changes to nested properties, deep reactivity is essential. The key is to understand the trade-offs and choose the approach that best fits your specific needs.

Conclusion: Becoming a Reactivity Architect

Understanding deep and shallow reactivity is crucial for building efficient and predictable Vue.js applications. By knowing how to create reactive data structures and how to choose the appropriate level of reactivity, you can create applications that respond dynamically to user input and server updates without sacrificing performance. By now you have all the information to become a pro on Vue's reactivity. This concludes our Reactivity deep dive.

Chapter 5: Introduction to the Composition API – A New Way to Organize Your Code

Welcome to a game-changing feature in Vue.js 3: the Composition API! In previous chapters, we've built our components using the Options API, which organizes component logic into predefined options like data, methods, computed, and watch. The Composition API, on the other hand, offers a more flexible and composable way to organize your component logic, especially as your applications grow in complexity.

Think of the Composition API as a way to structure your code in a modular and reusable way. It's like organizing your kitchen with separate drawers for utensils, cookware, and spices, rather than throwing everything into one big mess. This modularity leads to cleaner, more maintainable, and more testable code.

5.1 The Motivation Behind the Composition API – Why Change a Good Thing?: Embracing the Future of Vue.js

For a long time, the Options API has been the go-to method for building Vue.js components. It's structured, relatively easy to learn, and has powered countless successful Vue projects. So, you might be wondering: Why introduce a completely new way of organizing components with the Composition API? Was there something fundamentally broken with the Options API?

The answer, in short, is no. The Options API isn't broken, but it does have limitations that become more apparent as your applications grow in size and complexity. The Composition API isn't about replacing the Options API entirely; it's about providing a more powerful and flexible alternative for managing complex component logic. It's like upgrading from a reliable sedan to a versatile SUV - both get you where you need to go, but the SUV offers more room, flexibility, and capabilities for tackling diverse terrain.

The Core Issue: Scalability and Maintainability

The primary motivation behind the Composition API is to improve the scalability and maintainability of Vue.js applications, particularly large and complex ones. With the Options API, component logic is organized into predefined options like data, methods, computed, and watch. While this structure works well for simple components, it can become challenging to manage as components grow larger and more complex.

Here's the key problem: Related pieces of code can be separated by unrelated code.

The Problem Explained: The Example of Feature Fragmentation

Imagine a component that handles user authentication, data fetching, and UI updates. With the Options API, you might have code related to data fetching scattered across the data, methods, and watch options. This makes it harder to understand the component's overall logic and to reuse the data fetching logic in other components.

This fragmentation of related code is known as *feature fragmentation.* It makes it harder to reason about the component's behavior, to debug issues, and to refactor the code.

The Power of Collocation: Grouping Related Code

The Composition API solves the problem of feature fragmentation by allowing you to group related logic together in functions. This is known as *collocation.*

With the Composition API, you can create functions that encapsulate specific pieces of functionality, such as data fetching, user authentication, or form validation. You can then import and use these functions in any component that needs them. This promotes code reuse, reduces duplication, and makes your code more modular and maintainable.

Mixins: A Previous Attempt at Reusability (and their Shortcomings)

In Vue 2, mixins were a common way to share logic between components. However, mixins have several limitations:

- **Naming Conflicts:** Mixins can easily lead to naming conflicts if multiple mixins define the same data property or method.
- **Implicit Dependencies:** It's not always clear which components depend on which mixins. This can make it harder to understand and maintain your code.

- **Lack of Encapsulation:** Mixins are merged directly into the component, which can make it harder to reason about the component's behavior.

Composables: The Modern Solution for Reusability

The Composition API introduces the concept of *composables*, which are functions that encapsulate reusable logic. Composables are similar to mixins, but they offer several advantages:

- **Explicit Dependencies:** Composables clearly declare their dependencies.
- **No Naming Conflicts:** Composables don't introduce any new properties or methods into the component's namespace, avoiding naming conflicts.
- **Better Encapsulation:** Composables encapsulate their logic and data, preventing them from interfering with other parts of the component.

TypeScript Friendliness: Embracing Static Typing

Another key motivation behind the Composition API is to improve TypeScript support. The Options API was not designed with TypeScript in mind, making it difficult to use with TypeScript and catch type errors early on.

The Composition API, on the other hand, is more type-friendly and provides better support for TypeScript. This makes it easier to write type-safe Vue.js applications and catch type errors during development.

Why Does TypeScript Matter?

TypeScript is a superset of JavaScript that adds static typing to the language. Static typing allows you to define the types of variables, parameters, and return values in your code. This allows the TypeScript compiler to catch type errors during development, before you even run your code.

Using TypeScript can significantly improve the quality and maintainability of your code, especially in large and complex projects.

The Tradeoffs: Learning Curve and Verbosity

The Composition API does have a steeper learning curve than the Options API. It also tends to be more verbose, especially for simple components.

However, the benefits of improved scalability, maintainability, reusability, and TypeScript support outweigh the drawbacks for most large and complex Vue.js applications.

Personal Insight: From Skeptic to Convert

I must admit, when I first heard about the Composition API, I was skeptical. I was comfortable with the Options API, and I wasn't convinced that a new way of organizing components was necessary.

However, as I started to use the Composition API on larger projects, I quickly realized its benefits. The ability to group related logic together in functions, to reuse logic across multiple components, and to write type-safe code with TypeScript made my development process much more efficient and enjoyable.

Conclusion: Embracing the Evolution

The Composition API is not about replacing the Options API entirely. It's about providing a more powerful and flexible tool for building complex Vue.js applications. By understanding the motivations behind the Composition API and its benefits, you can make informed decisions about when and how to use it in your projects. In the next section, we'll get practical.

5.2 Setting Up the setup() Function – The Entry Point for Logic: Your Component's Command Center

We've talked about *why* the Composition API exists; now it's time to get practical and explore *how* to use it. At the heart of every component leveraging the Composition API lies the setup() function. Think of setup() as the command center of your component, the place where you define your reactive state, methods, computed properties, and lifecycle hooks. It's where all the action happens.

The setup() function is executed *before* the component is created, and it provides a way to initialize the component's state and logic before the template is rendered. It's the first thing that runs when Vue is trying to create a component.

The setup() Function: A Required Ingredient for Composition API

Every component that leverages the Composition API *must* have a setup() function. Without it, your Composition API-based code won't work!

Basic Structure: Defining Your Command Center

Here's the basic structure of a component using the setup() function:

```
      import { ref } from 'vue';

export default {
  setup() {
    // 1. Define reactive state, computed properties, and
methods here

    // 2. Return an object exposing the state and methods to
the template
    return {
      // reactiveState,
      // computedProperty,
      // method
    };
  },
  template: `
    <div>
      <!-- Use reactive state, computed properties, and
methods here -->
    </div>
  `
};
```

Key Steps:

1. **Import Necessary Functions:** Import any necessary functions from the vue module, such as ref, reactive, computed, watch, and lifecycle hooks. These are the tools in your toolbox.
2. **Define Reactive State, Computed Properties, and Methods:** Inside the setup() function, define your component's reactive state using ref and reactive, your computed properties using computed, and your methods using regular JavaScript functions. We'll explore these in more detail in the following sections.

3. **Return an Object:** Return an object from the setup() function. This object should contain all the reactive state, computed properties, and methods that you want to make available in your component's template. Anything you *don't* return will be hidden from the template.

Exposing to the Template: Making Data Accessible

Anything you want to use in your component's template *must* be returned from the setup() function. This includes:

- Reactive data properties (created with ref or reactive)
- Computed properties
- Methods

You return these values as properties of an object:

```
    import { ref } from 'vue';

export default {
  setup() {
    const count = ref(0);
    const message = ref('Hello!');

    const increment = () => {
      count.value++;
    };

    return {
      count,
      message,
      increment // Make methods available to the template
    };
  },
  template: `
    <div>
      <p>Count: {{ count }}</p>
      <p>Message: {{ message }}</p>
      <button @click="increment">Increment</button>
    </div>
  `
};
```

In this example, we're returning the count ref, the message ref, and the increment method from the setup() function. This makes them available in the component's template, where we can display the count and message and call the increment method when the button is clicked.

No this Keyword: A Different Context

Inside the setup() function, you *do not* have access to the this keyword. This is a fundamental difference between the Options API and the Composition API. In the Options API, you can access the component instance using this, but in the Composition API, you don't have access to the component instance in the setup() function.

This is because the setup() function is executed *before* the component is created. Vue does this so that you have an opportunity to define all of the reactive data before mounting the component.

Accessing the Component Instance: Lifecycle Hooks to the Rescue

If you need to access the component instance, you can use lifecycle hooks, which we'll discuss later. Lifecycle hooks are functions that are called at specific stages of a component's lifecycle, such as when the component is created, mounted, updated, or unmounted. Lifecycle hooks *do* have access to the component instance through the this keyword.

Understanding setup Arguments: The Props and Context

The setup function *can* accept two optional arguments:

1. **props:** An object containing the component's props.
2. **context:** An object that provides access to the component's context, including the attrs, emit, and slots properties.

Here's an example of how to access the props and context in the setup function:

```
    import { ref } from 'vue';

export default {
  props: {
    message: {
      type: String,
      required: true
    }
  },
  setup(props, context) {
```

```
    const count = ref(0);

    const increment = () => {
      count.value++;
      context.emit('increment', count.value); // Emit an
event
    };

    console.log(props.message); // Access the message prop
    console.log(context.attrs); // Access the attributes
passed to the component
    console.log(context.slots); // Access the slots passed to
the component

    return {
      count,
      increment
    };
  },
  template: `
    <div>
      <p>{{ props.message }}</p>
      <p>Count: {{ count }}</p>
      <button @click="increment">Increment</button>
    </div>
  `
};
```

Explanation:

- **props:** You receive an object containing the props you have defined with props: { ... }.
- **context:** You receive an object containing:
  - attrs: All attributes that you passed to the component.
  - emit: The function to emit data, just like this.$emit().
  - slots: All slots that you passed to the component.

A Complete Example: Building a Customizable Greeting Component

Let's create a complete example of a customizable greeting component using the Composition API:

```
      <!DOCTYPE html>
<html>
<head>
  <title>Greeting Component</title>
```

```
  <script
src="https://unpkg.com/vue@3/dist/vue.global.js"></script>
</head>
<body>
  <div id="app">
    <greeting-component name="John"
message="Welcome!"></greeting-component>
  </div>

  <script>
    const { createApp, ref } = Vue;

    const GreetingComponent = {
      props: {
        name: {
          type: String,
          required: true
        },
        message: {
          type: String,
          default: 'Hello'
        }
      },
      setup(props) {
        const greeting = ref(`${props.message},
${props.name}!`);

        return {
          greeting
        };
      },
      template: `
        <div>
          <h2>{{ greeting }}</h2>
        </div>
      `
    };

    const app = createApp({
      components: {
        GreetingComponent
      }
    });

    app.mount('#app');
  </script>
</body>
</html>
```

In this example, we define a GreetingComponent that accepts name and message props. The setup() function initializes a greeting ref with a customized greeting message using the props. The greeting ref is then made available in the component's template.

Personal Insight: setup(): A Paradigm Shift

Initially, I found the setup() function a bit strange, as it felt different from the way I was used to building components with the Options API. But once I embraced the new paradigm and started thinking in terms of composable functions, I found that the setup() function provided a much more organized and flexible way to structure my component logic.

Conclusion: Mastering the Command Center

The setup() function is the essential entry point for defining the logic of your Vue.js components when using the Composition API. With the setup function we start setting the stage for a Vue symphony to be created. By understanding how to use the setup function, how to access props and context, and how to return reactive state, computed properties, and methods, you can build more powerful and maintainable Vue.js applications.

5.3 Reactivity with ref and reactive (Composition API) – The Core of the System: Making Your Data Alive in Composition Components

In the previous section, we established the setup() function as the central hub for component logic when using the Composition API. Now, let's delve into the heart of making that logic reactive: the ref and reactive primitives. Just like the Options API, these primitives are essential for creating data that automatically updates your user interface when it changes. The Composition API uses these in the setup to enable components to keep track of data.

Think of ref and reactive as the lifeblood of your Composition API components. They're what makes your data dynamic and responsive, allowing your user interfaces to react intelligently to user interactions and data updates.

The Dynamic Duo: ref and reactive

Vue.js 3 provides two primary ways to create reactive data within the setup() function:

- **ref:** Used for creating reactive references to single, primitive values (numbers, strings, booleans, etc.) and any value (such as an array or object) that you intend to replace entirely. A ref holds a single value that can be accessed and modified through its .value property.
- **reactive:** Used for creating reactive objects and arrays. reactive makes all the properties of the object or array reactive, meaning that any changes to those properties will trigger updates in the DOM. Use this for tracking changes inside objects.

Why Two Different Primitives?

The existence of both ref and reactive might seem redundant at first, but they serve distinct purposes and are designed to handle different types of data and usage patterns.

- ref is designed for holding single values and for providing a way to replace the entire value with a new one.
- reactive is designed for making the *properties* of an object reactive, allowing you to modify the object in place.

Using ref in the setup() Function: Reactivity for Primitives and Replacements

To create a reactive reference to a primitive value using ref, you simply pass the initial value to the ref function:

```
      import { ref } from 'vue';

export default {
  setup() {
    const count = ref(0); // Create a reactive reference to a
number
    const message = ref('Hello!'); // Create a reactive
reference to a string
    const isLoggedIn = ref(false); // Create a reactive
reference to a boolean

    return {
      count,
      message,
      isLoggedIn
    };
```

```
  },
  template: `
    <div>
      <p>Count: {{ count }}</p>
      <p>Message: {{ message }}</p>
      <p>Is Logged In: {{ isLoggedIn }}</p>
    </div>
  `
};
```

Accessing and Modifying ref Values: The .value Property

To access or modify the value of a ref, you *must* use the .value property in your JavaScript code:

```
      import { ref } from 'vue';

export default {
  setup() {
    const count = ref(0);

    const increment = () => {
      count.value++; // Access and modify the value using
.value
    };

    return {
      count,
      increment
    };
  },
  template: `
    <div>
      <p>Count: {{ count }}</p>
      <button @click="increment">Increment</button>
    </div>
  `
};
```

Template Auto-Unwrapping: The Magic of Simplicity

Inside your component's template, you *don't* need to use the .value property to access ref values. Vue.js automatically unwraps refs in templates, making them easier to use:

```
      <template>
```

```
  <div>
    <p>Count: {{ count }}</p>  <!-- No .value needed here! --
>
    <button @click="increment">Increment</button>
  </div>
</template>
```

Using reactive in the setup() Function: Reactivity for Objects and Arrays

To create a reactive object or array using reactive, you simply pass the object or array to the reactive function:

```
      import { reactive } from 'vue';

export default {
  setup() {
    const state = reactive({
      name: 'John Doe',
      age: 30
    });

    const items = reactive(['Apple', 'Banana', 'Orange']);

    return {
      state,
      items
    };
  },
  template: `
    <div>
      <p>Name: {{ state.name }}</p>
      <p>Age: {{ state.age }}</p>
      <ul>
        <li v-for="item in items" :key="item">{{ item }}</li>
      </ul>
    </div>
  `
};
```

Accessing and Modifying reactive Properties: Standard JavaScript Syntax

To access or modify the properties of a reactive object, you use the standard dot notation or bracket notation:

```
import { reactive } from 'vue';

export default {
  setup() {
    const state = reactive({
      name: 'John Doe',
      age: 30
    });

    const updateName = (newName) => {
      state.name = newName; // Modify the name property
directly
    };

    return {
      state,
      updateName
    };
  },
  template: `
    <div>
      <p>Name: {{ state.name }}</p>
      <button @click="updateName('Jane Doe')">Update
Name</button>
    </div>
  `
};
```

Key Considerations for reactive:

- **Primitives Must Be Wrapped:** You cannot pass primitive values directly to reactive. If you need to make a primitive value reactive, wrap it in an object:

```
const state = reactive({
  count: 0 // Correct: count is a property of an object
});
```

- **No Complete Object Replacement:** Replacing a reactive object with a completely new object will break the reactivity. You should only modify the *properties* of the reactive object, not the object itself. Use ref instead to maintain reactivity.
- **Shallow Reactivity By Default:** reactive is *shallowly* reactive. It makes the top-level properties of the object reactive, but it doesn't automatically make nested objects or arrays reactive. We'll learn how to handle this in a later section.

Practical Example: A Dynamic To-Do List

Let's create a practical example of a dynamic to-do list using ref and reactive in the Composition API:

```
<template>
  <div>
    <h1>To-Do List</h1>
    <input type="text" v-model="newTodo"
@keyup.enter="addTodo" placeholder="Add a to-do...">
    <ul>
      <li v-for="todo in todos" :key="todo.id">{{ todo.text
}}</li>
    </ul>
  </div>
</template>

<script>
import { ref, reactive } from 'vue';

export default {
  setup() {
    const newTodo = ref('');
    const todos = reactive([]);

    const addTodo = () => {
      if (newTodo.value.trim() !== '') {
        todos.push({ id: Date.now(), text: newTodo.value });
        newTodo.value = '';
      }
    };

    return {
      newTodo,
      todos,
      addTodo
    };
  }
};
</script>
```

Explanation:

- newTodo is a ref that holds the value of the input field.
- todos is a reactive array that holds the list of to-do items.
- The addTodo method adds a new to-do item to the todos array and clears the input field.

Personal Insight: Mastering the ref/reactive Decision

It took me some time to internalize the best practices for choosing between ref and reactive. Initially, I would often default to reactive for everything. However, I quickly realized that ref is often the better choice for simple values and for situations where you need to replace the entire value.

Conclusion: The Power of Two – Harnessing ref and reactive

ref and reactive are the core building blocks of reactivity in the Composition API. By understanding how to use them effectively, you can create dynamic and responsive Vue.js applications. In the next section, we'll explore how to derive data using computed properties.

5.4 Computed Properties and Watchers (Composition API) – Responding to Changes: Beyond Raw Data - Reacting to Derived State and Side Effects

We've seen how ref and reactive let us create data in our components. That's great, but what do we do with that data? How do we respond to changes in it? That's where computed and watch come in to play. Computed Properties and Watchers let us create dynamic UIs and have side effects.

Think of computed as creating a dependent result, and watch as setting up a response.

Computed Properties: Efficiently Deriving Data

Computed properties are a powerful way to derive new data from existing reactive data. They're functions that automatically recalculate their value whenever their dependencies change. This ensures that your data stays consistent and up-to-date. A computed property returns a calculated value that you can then easily call.

In the Composition API, you define computed properties using the computed function from Vue.js:

```
      import { ref, computed } from 'vue';

export default {
  setup() {
```

```
    const firstName = ref('John');
    const lastName = ref('Doe');

    const fullName = computed(() => {
      return firstName.value + ' ' + lastName.value;
    });

    return {
      firstName,
      lastName,
      fullName
    };
  },
  template: `
    <div>
      <p>Full Name: {{ fullName }}</p>
    </div>
  `
};
```

Key Points:

- **Dependency Tracking:** Vue automatically tracks the reactive data used inside the computed function. Vue updates this computed property's value automatically.
- **Caching:** Vue will not run the code if the source data has not been modified, this caching makes things very performant.

Why Use Computed Properties Instead of Methods?

While you could technically achieve the same result by calling a method in your template, computed properties offer several advantages:

- **Caching:** As mentioned earlier, computed properties are cached, which can significantly improve performance.
- **Declarative Nature:** Computed properties clearly express the relationship between the derived data and its dependencies, making your code easier to understand and maintain. The result of a function isn't clear right away, with computed properties, that is immediately apparent.

Practical Example: Calculating a Shopping Cart Total

Let's revisit our shopping cart example from the previous section and use a computed property to calculate the total value of the cart:

```
    <template>
  <div>
    <h2>Shopping Cart</h2>
    <ul>
      <li v-for="item in cart" :key="item.id">
        {{ item.name }} - ${{ item.price }} - Quantity: {{
item.quantity }}
      </li>
    </ul>
    <h3>Total: ${{ cartTotal }}</h3>
  </div>
</template>

<script>
import { ref, computed } from 'vue';

export default {
  setup() {
    const cart = ref([
      { id: 1, name: 'Product A', price: 10, quantity: 2 },
      { id: 2, name: 'Product B', price: 20, quantity: 1 }
    ]);

    const cartTotal = computed(() => {
      return cart.value.reduce((total, item) => {
        return total + item.price * item.quantity;
      }, 0);
    });

    return {
      cart,
      cartTotal
    };
  }
};
</script>
```

Here, the cartTotal computed property depends on the cart ref. Whenever the cart ref changes, the cartTotal computed property will be automatically recalculated.

Read-Only and Writable Computed Properties: Gettings and Settings

The above example is great, but what happens if you want to update one of the source values? You may have thought that the computed properties are the source of truth, but they are just a reflection! For that we will need to tell the computer property to use a setter:

```
      import { ref, computed } from 'vue';

export default {
  setup() {
    const firstName = ref('John')
    const lastName = ref('Doe')

    const fullName = computed({
      get() {
        return `${firstName.value} ${lastName.value}`
      },
      set(newValue) {
        // Note: we are using destructuring assignment here
        [firstName.value, lastName.value] = newValue.split('
')
      }
    })

    return {
      firstName,
      lastName,
      fullName
    }
  },
  template: `
    <p>Fullname is: {{fullName}}</p>

    <input type="text" v-model="fullName">
  `
}
```

Watchers: Responding to Data Changes with Side Effects

While computed properties are excellent for deriving data, watchers are designed for performing *side effects* in response to data changes. A side effect is any operation that interacts with the outside world, such as making an API call, updating a local storage value, or logging a message to the console.

In the Composition API, you define watchers using the watch function from Vue.js.

```
        import { ref, watch } from 'vue';

export default {
  setup() {
    const inputValue = ref('');

    watch(
      inputValue,
      (newValue, oldValue) => {
        console.log(`inputValue changed from ${oldValue} to
${newValue}`);
        // Perform a side effect, like making an API call
      }
    );

    return {
      inputValue
    };
  },
  template: `
    <div>
      <input type="text" v-model="inputValue">
    </div>
  `
};
```

Key Points:

- **Source:** The first argument to watch is the data property you want to watch. It can be a ref, a reactive property, or a getter function.
- **Callback:** The second argument is a callback function that is executed whenever the data property changes. The callback function receives the new value and the old value as arguments.

Practical Example: Making an API Call When Data Changes

Let's create a practical example of making an API call whenever a search term changes:

```
        <template>
  <div>
    <input type="text" v-model="searchTerm"
placeholder="Search...">
  </div>
</template>

<script>
```

```
import { ref, watch } from 'vue';

export default {
  setup() {
    const searchTerm = ref('');

    const fetchData = async (term) => {
      console.log(`Fetching data for search term: ${term}`);
      // Simulate an API call
      await new Promise(resolve => setTimeout(resolve, 500));
      console.log(`Data fetched for search term: ${term}`);
    };

    watch(
      searchTerm,
      (newValue) => {
        fetchData(newValue);
      }
    );

    return {
      searchTerm
    };
  }
};
</script>
```

In this example, we're watching the searchTerm ref. Whenever the searchTerm changes, we call the fetchData function to make an API call.

Watch Options: Controlling Watcher Behavior

The watch function also accepts an optional third argument: an options object that allows you to configure the watcher's behavior:

- **immediate: true:** This option causes the callback function to be executed immediately when the watcher is created, before any data changes have occurred.
- **deep: true:** This option enables deep watching. When deep is set to true, the watcher will also track changes to nested properties within objects and arrays.

watchEffect: A Streamlined Approach to Watchers

Vue also offers watchEffect, which makes dependency tracking even easier by auto-detecting dependencies within the executed code,

```
    import { ref, watchEffect } from 'vue'

export default {
  setup() {
    const message = ref('Hello')

    watchEffect(() => {
      console.log('New value is', message.value)
    })

    return {
      message
    }
  },
  template: `
    <input type="text" v-model="message" />
  `
}
```

Personal Insight: When to Computed and When to Watch

I originally was unsure as to when to use what. The key difference for me was this:

- **Use Computed for Data Transformation:**
- **Use Watch for side effects.**

Conclusion: Harnessing the Power of Reactivity

Computed properties and watchers are essential tools for building dynamic and responsive Vue.js applications. By understanding how to use them effectively, you can create applications that react intelligently to user input and server updates. I hope this overview has given you an appreciation for the power of Vue to make changes to data easy to detect.

5.5 Lifecycle Hooks (Composition API) – Tapping into Key Moments: Orchestrating Your Component's Journey

Every Vue.js component goes through a series of stages during its lifetime, from its initial creation to its eventual destruction. These stages are known as *lifecycle hooks*. Lifecycle hooks provide opportunities to execute code at specific points in a component's lifecycle, allowing you to perform tasks such as initializing data, making API calls, setting up event listeners, and cleaning up resources.

In the Options API, lifecycle hooks are defined as options on the component object (e.g., mounted, updated, unmounted). In the Composition API, lifecycle hooks are accessed using functions that start with on, such as onMounted, onUpdated, and onUnmounted. This change may seem subtle, but has powerful implications in making the code grouped and maintainable.

Think of lifecycle hooks as checkpoints along a component's journey. Each checkpoint represents a specific stage in the component's lifecycle, and you can place code at these checkpoints to perform specific actions. They are an amazing tool to group specific related actions at certain points.

The Key Lifecycle Hooks in the Composition API

Here's a rundown of the most commonly used lifecycle hooks in the Composition API:

- **onBeforeMount:** Called right before the component is about to mount to the DOM. At this point, the template has been compiled, but the component has not yet been inserted into the DOM. You can access the data and computed properties, but you cannot access the DOM elements.
- **onMounted:** Called after the component has been mounted to the DOM. At this point, the component has been inserted into the DOM, and you can access the DOM elements. This is a great place to perform tasks that require access to the DOM, such as setting up event listeners or initializing third-party libraries.
- **onBeforeUpdate:** Called right before the component is about to update its DOM due to a data change. This hook allows you to access the DOM state right before Vue is about to re-render the DOM.
- **onUpdated:** Called after the component has updated its DOM due to a data change. Similar to onMounted, this can be used to perform DOM-related operations.
- **onBeforeUnmount:** Called right before the component is about to be unmounted from the DOM. This hook allows you to perform cleanup tasks, such as removing event listeners or canceling timers.
- **onUnmounted:** Called after the component has been unmounted from the DOM. At this point, the component has been removed from the DOM, and you should no longer access any DOM elements.

- **onErrorCaptured:** Called when an error from any child component has been caught. You can use this to gracefully handle the error, display a fallback UI, or log the error to a server.
- **onRenderTracked:** Called when a reactive dependency is tracked during the component's render process. This is useful for debugging performance issues.
- **onRenderTriggered:** Called when the component's render function is triggered due to a dependency change. This is also useful for debugging performance issues.

Accessing Lifecycle Hooks: The on Functions

To access lifecycle hooks in the Composition API, you use functions that start with on, followed by the name of the lifecycle hook (e.g., onMounted, onUpdated, onUnmounted). These functions take a callback function as their argument, which will be executed when the corresponding lifecycle hook is triggered.

```
import { onMounted } from 'vue';

export default {
  setup() {
    onMounted(() => {
      console.log('Component mounted!');
    });

    return {
      // ...
    };
  },
  template: `
    <div>
      <!-- ... -->
    </div>
  `
};
```

The Execution Context: Inside the setup() Function

Lifecycle hook functions must be called *synchronously* within the setup() function. Calling them asynchronously or outside of the setup() function will not work.

Practical Examples: Putting Lifecycle Hooks to Use

Let's explore some practical examples of how to use lifecycle hooks in the Composition API:

1. Making an API Call on Mount:

```
    <template>
  <div>
    <p v-if="loading">Loading...</p>
    <ul v-else>
      <li v-for="item in items" :key="item.id">{{ item.name
}}</li>
    </ul>
  </div>
</template>

<script>
import { ref, onMounted } from 'vue';

export default {
  setup() {
    const items = ref([]);
    const loading = ref(true);

    onMounted(async () => {
      try {
        // Simulate an API call
        const data = await new Promise(resolve => {
          setTimeout(() => {
            resolve([
              { id: 1, name: 'Item 1' },
              { id: 2, name: 'Item 2' }
            ]);
          }, 1000);
        });

        items.value = data;
      } finally {
        loading.value = false;
      }
    });

    return {
      items,
      loading
    };
  }
};
</script>
```

In this example, we use the onMounted hook to make an API call after the component has been mounted to the DOM. We set a loading flag to display a loading indicator while the data is being fetched.

2. Setting Up and Tearing Down Event Listeners:

```
    <template>
  <div>
    <p>Mouse Position: {{ x }}, {{ y }}</p>
  </div>
</template>

<script>
import { ref, onMounted, onUnmounted } from 'vue';

export default {
  setup() {
    const x = ref(0);
    const y = ref(0);

    const updateMousePosition = (event) => {
      x.value = event.clientX;
      y.value = event.clientY;
    };

    onMounted(() => {
      window.addEventListener('mousemove',
updateMousePosition);
    });

    onUnmounted(() => {
      window.removeEventListener('mousemove',
updateMousePosition);
    });

    return {
      x,
      y
    };
  }
};
</script>
```

In this example, we use the onMounted hook to add a mousemove event listener to the window. We use the onUnmounted hook to remove the event listener when the component is unmounted. This prevents memory leaks and ensures that the event listener is only active when the component is visible.

3. Managing Resources: Tying to a Component's Life

Lifecycle hooks are a perfect place to setup and manage a resource that may exist on a third party.

```
      <template>
  <div>
    <h2>{{ msg }}</h2>
  </div>
</template>

<script>
import { ref, onMounted, onUnmounted } from 'vue'
import * as THREE from 'three'

export default {
  setup() {
    const msg = ref('This is three js message')
    let scene, camera, renderer, geometry, material, mesh

    onMounted(() => {
      scene = new THREE.Scene()
      camera = new THREE.PerspectiveCamera(
        75,
        window.innerWidth / window.innerHeight,
        0.1,
        1000
      )

      renderer = new THREE.WebGLRenderer({
        antialias: true,
        alpha: true
      })

      renderer.setSize(window.innerWidth, window.innerHeight)
      renderer.setClearColor(0x000000, 0)
      document.body.appendChild(renderer.domElement)

      geometry = new THREE.BoxGeometry(1, 1, 1)
      material = new THREE.MeshBasicMaterial({ color:
0x00ff00 })
      mesh = new THREE.Mesh(geometry, material)
      scene.add(mesh)

      camera.position.z = 5

      const animate = () => {
        requestAnimationFrame(animate)

        mesh.rotation.x += 0.01
```

```
        mesh.rotation.y += 0.01

        renderer.render(scene, camera)
      }

      animate()
    })

    onUnmounted(() => {
      renderer.dispose()
      geometry.dispose()
      material.dispose()
    })

    return {
      msg
    }
  }
}
</script>

<style scoped>
h2 {
  color: white;
}
</style>
```

Personal Insight: Lifecycle Hooks - A Crucial Connection

I initially struggled to fully appreciate the power of lifecycle hooks. They seemed like just another set of functions to memorize. However, once I started using them to manage resources, make API calls, and set up event listeners, I realized how essential they are for building robust and well-behaved Vue.js applications.

Conclusion: Orchestrating Your Component's Journey

Lifecycle hooks are essential tools for managing the behavior of your Vue.js components throughout their lifetime. By understanding how to use the onMounted, onUpdated, onUnmounted, and other lifecycle hooks, you can create components that are well-behaved, efficient, and responsive to changes in the application environment. This concludes our Intro to Composition API, now onto advanced topics!

Chapter 6: Advanced Composition API Techniques – Taking Your Skills to the Next Level

In the previous chapter, we introduced the Composition API and covered the fundamentals of creating reactive components using setup(), ref, reactive, computed, watch, and lifecycle hooks. Now, it's time to delve into more advanced techniques that will unlock the full potential of the Composition API and enable you to build more scalable, maintainable, and testable Vue.js applications.

This chapter is all about taking your Composition API skills to the next level. We'll explore how to create reusable composables, how to use dependency injection to share data between components, how to handle asynchronous operations effectively, and how to leverage the power of TypeScript with the Composition API.

6.1 Creating Reusable Composables – Extracting Logic for Maximum Reuse: The DRY Principle in Action

We've established the power and flexibility of the Composition API. Now, let's explore a critical pattern that elevates its potential: *composables*. Composables are the secret sauce for building scalable, maintainable, and DRY (Don't Repeat Yourself) Vue.js applications.

Composables are functions that encapsulate a piece of reusable logic. They typically manage some reactive state, and they can also include methods, computed properties, and lifecycle hooks. The beauty of composables is that they can be imported and used in multiple components, allowing you to share logic across your entire application without duplicating code.

Think of composables as custom hooks or mini-utilities tailored for Vue.js. They represent a powerful shift from a component-centric view, to a function-centric view. They extract shared code into a module that can be used by any function that needs it.

Why Composables? The Benefits of Reusable Logic

- **DRY Principle:** Eliminates code duplication by extracting common logic into reusable functions.

- **Improved Maintainability:** Changes to reusable logic only need to be made in one place, rather than in multiple components.
- **Increased Testability:** Composables can be tested in isolation, making it easier to ensure that they are working correctly.
- **Enhanced Code Organization:** By extracting complex logic into composables, you can keep your components clean and focused on their primary responsibilities.
- **Clear separation of concerns:** You can now keep unrelated code in separate composables, without them getting in each other's way.

The use Prefix: Convention Over Configuration

It's a widely accepted convention to name composables with the use prefix (e.g., useMousePosition, useTheme, useFetch). This makes it easy to identify composables in your codebase and to distinguish them from other functions.

Creating a Composable: A Step-by-Step Guide

Here's a step-by-step guide to creating a composable:

1. **Identify Reusable Logic:** Identify a piece of logic that is used in multiple components or that is likely to be reused in the future.
2. **Create a New JavaScript File:** Create a new JavaScript file for your composable (e.g., useMousePosition.js).
3. **Define the Composable Function:** Define a function that encapsulates the reusable logic. This function should:
   - Import any necessary functions from Vue.js (e.g., ref, reactive, onMounted, onUnmounted).
   - Define reactive state using ref and reactive.
   - Define any necessary methods.
   - Use lifecycle hooks to perform any setup or cleanup tasks.
   - Return an object containing the reactive state and methods that you want to expose.
4. **Export the Composable Function:** Export the composable function so that it can be imported and used in other components.

A Practical Example: The useMousePosition Composable

Let's revisit our useMousePosition example from the previous section and create a reusable composable:

```
// useMousePosition.js
```

```
import { ref, onMounted, onUnmounted } from 'vue';

export function useMousePosition() {
  const x = ref(0);
  const y = ref(0);

  const updateMousePosition = (event) => {
    x.value = event.clientX;
    y.value = event.clientY;
  };

  onMounted(() => {
    window.addEventListener('mousemove',
updateMousePosition);
  });

  onUnmounted(() => {
    window.removeEventListener('mousemove',
updateMousePosition);
  });

  return {
    x,
    y
  };
}
```

Using the Composable: Integrating Reusable Logic into Your Components

To use a composable in a component, you simply import it and call it within the setup() function:

```
      <template>
  <div>
    <p>Mouse Position: {{ x }}, {{ y }}</p>
  </div>
</template>

<script>
import { useMousePosition } from './useMousePosition';

export default {
  setup() {
    const { x, y } = useMousePosition();

    return {
      x,
      y
```

```
    };
  }
};
</script>
```

Key Steps:

1. **Import the Composable:** Import the composable function from its file.
2. **Call the Composable:** Call the composable function within the setup() function.
3. **Destructure the Return Value:** Destructure the object returned by the composable to access the reactive state and methods.
4. **Return from setup():** Return the destructured values from the setup() function to make them available in the template.

Personal Insight: Composables: A Game-Changer for Large Projects

Composables have been a game-changer for building large and complex Vue.js applications. They've allowed me to extract common logic into reusable functions, making my code more organized, maintainable, and testable.

Advanced Techniques: Composables Calling Composables

Composables can call each other! This allows you to create highly composable and modular logic.

```
import { ref, computed } from 'vue';

function useCounter(initialValue = 0) {
  const count = ref(initialValue);

  function increment() {
    count.value++;
  }

  function decrement() {
    count.value--;
  }

  return {
    count,
    increment,
    decrement
```

```
  };
}

function useDoubleCounter(initialValue = 0) {
  const { count, increment, decrement } =
useCounter(initialValue);

  const double = computed(() => count.value * 2);

  return {
    count,
    double,
    increment,
    decrement
  };
}
```

Why Are Composables Better Than Mixins?

Composables address the problems that Mixins originally had:

- **Naming Collisions:** Composables make the properties explicit, and do not randomly merge, so naming collisions are no longer an issue.
- **Clear Source:** Its clear to see where a composable comes from (simply using an import).

Practical Example: A Theme Toggle with Local Storage Persistence

Let's enhance our theme toggle example from the previous section and create a composable that persists the theme to local storage:

```
      // useLocalStorage.js
import { ref, watch } from 'vue';

export function useLocalStorage(key, initialValue) {
  const storedValue = localStorage.getItem(key);
  const value = ref(storedValue || initialValue);

  watch(value, (newValue) => {
    localStorage.setItem(key, newValue);
  });

  return value;
}

// useTheme.js
import { useLocalStorage } from './useLocalStorage';
```

```
export function useTheme() {
  const theme = useLocalStorage('theme', 'light');

  const toggleTheme = () => {
    theme.value = theme.value === 'light' ? 'dark' : 'light';
    document.documentElement.setAttribute('data-theme',
theme.value);
  };

  onMounted(() => {
    document.documentElement.setAttribute('data-theme',
theme.value);
  });

  return {
    theme,
    toggleTheme
  };
}
```

In this example, we've created a useLocalStorage composable that encapsulates the logic for storing and retrieving data from local storage. The useTheme composable uses the useLocalStorage composable to persist the theme to local storage.

Key Takeaways:

- Composables are functions that encapsulate reusable logic.
- They promote code reuse, improve maintainability, and increase testability.
- Use the use prefix to name your composables.
- Import and call composables within the setup() function.
- Destructure the return value of composables to access the reactive state and methods.

Conclusion: Mastering the Art of Composability

Creating reusable composables is a key skill for building scalable and maintainable Vue.js applications. By following the principles and techniques outlined in this section, you can create a codebase that is organized, efficient, and easy to understand. In the next section, we'll learn about Depency Injection.

6.2 Dependency Injection (provide/inject) – Sharing Data Across Components: Beyond Props - Providing Data Down the Component Tree

In complex Vue.js applications, you'll often encounter situations where you need to share data between components that are not directly related. Passing data down through props at every level can become cumbersome and lead to prop drilling—the tedious process of passing props through intermediate components that don't actually need them. Dependency injection provides a powerful alternative, allowing you to share data between components without explicitly passing it down through props.

Think of dependency injection as creating a "global" data scope within a portion of your component tree. A parent component can *provide* data to this scope, and any descendant component can *inject* that data, regardless of its position in the component tree. This eliminates the need for prop drilling and makes your code more modular and maintainable.

The Foundation: The provide and inject Functions

Vue.js provides two primary functions for implementing dependency injection:

- **provide:** Used in a parent component to provide data to its descendants. The component providing the data is often an application-level component.
- **inject:** Used in a descendant component to inject data provided by an ancestor component.

Providing Data: The Parent's Role with provide

To provide data to its descendants, a component uses the provide function within its setup() function. Provide requires a key and then the data being passed down the component tree.

```
    import { ref, provide } from 'vue';

export default {
  setup() {
    const message = ref('Hello from the provider!');

    provide('message', message); // Provide the message data
```

```
    return {
      // ...
    };
  },
  template: `
    <div>
      <!-- ... -->
    </div>
  `
};
```

In this example, we're providing the message ref to all descendants of this component. Any descendant component can now inject the message using the key we've provided - 'message'.

Injecting Data: The Child's Perspective with inject

To inject data provided by an ancestor component, a descendant component uses the inject function within its setup() function. The key must exactly match the value defined in provide.

```
      import { inject } from 'vue';

export default {
  setup() {
    const message = inject('message'); // Inject the message
data

    return {
      message
    };
  },
  template: `
    <div>
      <p>{{ message }}</p>  <!-- Use the injected message -->
    </div>
  `
};
```

In this example, we're injecting the message data that was provided by an ancestor component using dependency injection. The child then calls the specific inject key: 'message' to then display the value.

Important Considerations

- **Key Matching:** The injection key used in inject must exactly match the key used in provide.
- **Optional Data:** By default, inject assumes the data is required. To inject data where a value is optional, set a default value using the following inject('message', 'default message');
- **Reactivity Maintained:** If you provide a ref or reactive object, the injected data will remain reactive, meaning that any changes to the data will be reflected in all components that are injecting it.
- **Symbol Keys:** For greater type safety and to avoid naming conflicts, consider using JavaScript Symbols as injection keys.
- **Not a Replacement for Props:** Dependency injection is not a replacement for props. It should be used for sharing data that is needed by many components throughout the application, such as configuration settings, user authentication state, or theme information. For passing data between parent and child components, props are still the preferred approach.

Practical Example: Sharing a Theme Object Throughout the App

Let's create a practical example of sharing a theme object throughout the app using dependency injection:

```
      // ThemeProvider.vue
<template>
  <slot />
</template>

<script>
import { reactive, provide } from 'vue'

export default {
  setup() {
    const theme = reactive({
      primaryColor: 'blue',
      secondaryColor: 'lightblue',
      textColor: 'black'
    })

    provide('theme', theme)

    return {}
  }
}
</script>
```

```
    //ComponentA.vue

<template>
  <div :style="themedStyles">
    This is Component A
  </div>
</template>

<script>
import { inject, computed } from 'vue'

export default {
  setup() {
    const theme = inject('theme')

    const themedStyles = computed(() => ({
      backgroundColor: theme.primaryColor,
      color: theme.textColor
    }))

    return { themedStyles }
  }
}
</script>

    //ComponentB.vue
<template>
  <div :style="themedStyles">
    This is Component B
  </div>
</template>

<script>
import { inject, computed } from 'vue'

export default {
  setup() {
    const theme = inject('theme')

    const themedStyles = computed(() => ({
      backgroundColor: theme.secondaryColor,
      color: theme.textColor
    }))

    return { themedStyles }
  }
}
</script>
```

In this example, the ThemeProvider component provides a theme object to all of its descendants. The ComponentA and ComponentB components inject the theme object and use its properties to style themselves. This allows you to easily change the theme of your entire application by simply updating the theme object in the ThemeProvider component. The template is then able to react to the value set in the inject

Personal Insight: Dependency Injection: A Key to Testability

One of the biggest benefits of dependency injection that I've discovered is its impact on testability. By using dependency injection, you can easily mock or stub dependencies during testing, allowing you to isolate and test your components in a controlled environment.

Conclusion: Sharing Made Easy

Dependency injection is a powerful tool for sharing data across components in Vue.js applications. By understanding how to use the provide and inject functions, you can create more modular, maintainable, and testable code. Be sure to compare with composition API which can often be another great choice when it comes to reusable logic.

6.3 Handling Asynchronous Operations: Keeping Your UI Responsive – Mastering the Art of Waiting (Gracefully)

Asynchronous operations are an unavoidable reality in modern web development. Whether you're fetching data from an API, processing images, or performing complex calculations, you'll often encounter tasks that take time to complete. If you're not careful, these asynchronous operations can block the main thread and make your UI unresponsive, leading to a poor user experience. This is why learning to handle asynchronous functions can make the biggest difference.

This section delves into techniques for handling asynchronous operations gracefully in Vue.js using the Composition API, ensuring that your UI remains responsive and your users stay engaged.

Understanding the Challenge: The Asynchronous Nature of the Web

JavaScript is inherently single-threaded, meaning that it can only execute one task at a time. When you perform an asynchronous operation, such as making an API call, JavaScript doesn't wait for the operation to complete before moving on to the next task. Instead, it registers a callback function that will be executed when the operation is finished.

If your callback function takes a long time to execute, it can block the main thread and prevent the browser from updating the UI, responding to user input, or performing other essential tasks. This is what causes the "freezing" or "unresponsiveness" that users sometimes experience when using web applications.

The Tools of the Trade: async/await and Promises

JavaScript provides two primary mechanisms for handling asynchronous operations:

- **Promises:** Promises represent the eventual result of an asynchronous operation. They provide a way to chain together multiple asynchronous operations and handle errors gracefully.
- **async/await:** The async/await syntax is syntactic sugar that makes it easier to write asynchronous code that looks and feels synchronous. It's built on top of Promises and provides a more readable and maintainable way to handle asynchronous operations.

In Vue.js, you'll typically use async/await in conjunction with Promises to handle asynchronous operations within your components.

A Step-by-Step Approach: Fetching Data with async/await

Let's walk through a step-by-step example of fetching data from an API using the Composition API and async/await:

1. **Define an Asynchronous Function:**

```
    const fetchData = async () => {
  try {
    // Make an API call using fetch or Axios
    const response = await
fetch('https://jsonplaceholder.typicode.com/todos/1');
    const data = await response.json();

    // Update the data property
    todo.value = data;
  } catch (error) {
    // Handle errors
```

```
    console.error('Error fetching data:', error);
    errorMessage.value = 'Failed to fetch data.';
  } finally {
    // Set loading to false
    loading.value = false;
  }
};
```

- Use the async keyword to declare the function as asynchronous.
- Use the await keyword to wait for the asynchronous operation to complete before moving on to the next line of code.
- Use a try...catch block to handle any errors that may occur during the asynchronous operation.
- Use a finally block to perform any cleanup tasks, such as setting the loading flag to false.

2. **Call the Asynchronous Function in a Lifecycle Hook:**

```
      import { ref, onMounted } from 'vue';

export default {
  setup() {
    const todo = ref(null);
    const loading = ref(true);
    const errorMessage = ref('');

    const fetchData = async () => { // The async function
from above
      try {
        // Make an API call using fetch or Axios
        const response = await
fetch('https://jsonplaceholder.typicode.com/todos/1');
        const data = await response.json();

        // Update the data property
        todo.value = data;
      } catch (error) {
        // Handle errors
        console.error('Error fetching data:', error);
        errorMessage.value = 'Failed to fetch data.';
      } finally {
        // Set loading to false
        loading.value = false;
      }
    };

    onMounted(fetchData); // Call the async function on mount
```

```
    return {
      todo,
      loading,
      errorMessage
    };
  }
};
```

- Call the asynchronous function within a lifecycle hook, such as onMounted. This ensures that the asynchronous operation is only performed after the component has been mounted to the DOM.

3. **Display a Loading Indicator:**

```
      <template>
  <div>
    <p v-if="loading">Loading...</p>
    <div v-else-if="errorMessage">Error: {{ errorMessage
}}</div>
    <div v-else>
      <h2>{{ todo.title }}</h2>
      <p>Completed: {{ todo.completed }}</p>
    </div>
  </div>
</template>
```

- Use a loading ref to display a loading indicator while the data is being fetched.
- Use an errorMessage ref to display an error message if the data fails to load.

Practical Considerations: Error Handling and User Feedback

- **Graceful Error Handling:** Always wrap your asynchronous operations in try...catch blocks to handle any errors that may occur. Display informative error messages to the user and consider providing options to retry the operation or contact support.
- **Meaningful Loading Indicators:** Use loading indicators to provide visual feedback to the user while the data is being fetched. This helps to prevent the user from thinking that the application is frozen or broken. Use loading spinners, progress bars, or skeleton screens to provide a visual representation of the loading progress.

- **Debouncing and Throttling:** For operations that are triggered frequently, such as typing in a search box, consider using debouncing or throttling to limit the number of times the operation is executed. Debouncing ensures that the operation is only executed after a certain period of inactivity, while throttling limits the rate at which the operation is executed.

Personal Insight: Asynchronous Operations: A Balancing Act

Handling asynchronous operations effectively is a balancing act between providing a responsive user interface and performing necessary tasks in the background. It requires careful planning and attention to detail to ensure that your application remains performant and user-friendly.

Practical Example: A Search Component with Debouncing

Let's create a practical example of a search component that uses debouncing to limit the number of API calls:

```
      <template>
  <div>
    <input type="text" v-model="searchTerm"
placeholder="Search...">
    <ul v-if="results.length > 0">
      <li v-for="result in results" :key="result.id">{{
result.title }}</li>
    </ul>
    <p v-else-if="searchTerm">No results found.</p>
  </div>
</template>

<script>
import { ref, watch } from 'vue';

export default {
  setup() {
    const searchTerm = ref('');
    const results = ref([]);

    const search = async (term) => {
      console.log(`Performing search for term: ${term}`);
      // Simulate an API call
      const data = await new Promise(resolve => {
        setTimeout(() => {
          resolve([
            { id: 1, title: `Result for ${term} 1` },
            { id: 2, title: `Result for ${term} 2` }
```

```
        ]);
      }, 500);
    });
    results.value = data;
  };

  const debouncedSearch = debounce(search, 500); //
Debounce for 500ms

  watch(searchTerm, (newValue) => {
    debouncedSearch(newValue);
  });

  // Debounce function
  function debounce(func, delay) {
    let timeoutId;
    return function(...args) {
      clearTimeout(timeoutId);
      timeoutId = setTimeout(() => {
        func.apply(this, args);
      }, delay);
    };
  }

  return {
    searchTerm,
    results
  };
 }
};
</script>
```

In this example, we use a debounce function to limit the number of times the search function is called. The debounce function ensures that the search function is only called after the user has stopped typing for 500 milliseconds. This prevents the application from making excessive API calls while the user is typing.

Conclusion: The Path to Responsive Applications

Handling asynchronous operations effectively is essential for building responsive and user-friendly Vue.js applications. By understanding how to use async/await, Promises, loading states, error handling, and debouncing, you can create applications that provide a smooth and engaging user experience, even when performing complex and time-consuming tasks. Let's move on to TypeScript.

6.4 Using the Composition API with TypeScript: Type-Safe Vue Components – Supercharging Your Code with TypeScript's Safety Net

While Vue.js is a powerful and flexible framework, JavaScript's dynamic nature can sometimes lead to runtime errors that are difficult to debug. TypeScript brings static typing to JavaScript, allowing you to define the types of variables, parameters, and return values in your code. This enables the TypeScript compiler to catch type errors during development, before you even run your code.

Combining the Composition API with TypeScript results in more robust, maintainable, and scalable Vue.js applications. The Composition API's explicit, function-based organization pairs incredibly well with TypeScript's type-checking capabilities. TypeScript helps you catch errors, and the composable function-based structure of the composition API helps keep the project maintainable.

Why TypeScript? The Benefits of Static Typing

- **Early Error Detection:** TypeScript can catch type errors during development, before you even run your code. This can save you a lot of time and effort in debugging.
- **Improved Code Maintainability:** Type annotations make your code easier to understand and maintain. They provide valuable documentation that describes the expected types of data.
- **Better Code Completion:** TypeScript provides better code completion and IntelliSense in your IDE, making it easier to write code.
- **Enhanced Refactoring:** TypeScript makes it easier to refactor your code with confidence, knowing that type errors will be caught early on.

Setting Up TypeScript with Vue.js: A Step-by-Step Guide

To use TypeScript with Vue.js, you'll need to set up a TypeScript project and configure Vue.js to use TypeScript. This typically involves the following steps:

1. **Create a Vue.js Project with TypeScript Support:**

You can create a new Vue.js project with TypeScript support using the Vue CLI:

```
vue create my-typescript-project
```

During the project creation process, you'll be prompted to choose a preset. Select the "Manually select features" option and make sure to select the "TypeScript" option.

2. **Install Dependencies:**

   Once the project is created, you'll need to install the necessary dependencies:

```
cd my-typescript-project
npm install
# OR
yarn install
```

3. **Configure TypeScript:**

   The Vue CLI will automatically create a tsconfig.json file in the root of your project. This file contains the TypeScript compiler options. You can customize these options to suit your needs.

Type Annotations: Adding Type Safety to Your Code

The key to using TypeScript effectively is to add type annotations to your code. Type annotations tell the TypeScript compiler what types of data to expect in your variables, parameters, and return values.

1. Type Annotations with ref:

To add type annotations to ref variables, you use the Ref type from the vue module:

```
import { ref, Ref } from 'vue';

const message: Ref<string> = ref('Hello!'); // Explicitly
type the ref
const count = ref<number>(0); // Explicitly type the ref
```

```
const isLoggedIn = ref<boolean>(false); // Explicitly type
the ref
```

- Ref<string>: This specifies that the message ref should hold a string value.
- ref<number>(0): Alternative shorthand.

2. Type Annotations with reactive:

To add type annotations to reactive objects, you define an interface or type alias that describes the structure of the object:

```
import { reactive } from 'vue';

interface User {
  name: string;
  age: number;
}

const user: User = reactive({
  name: 'John Doe',
  age: 30
});
```

- We define a User interface that specifies the expected properties of the user object.
- We use the User interface as a type annotation for the user variable.

3. Type Annotations with Computed Properties:

When declaring a computed value, you can make the return type even more concrete:

```
import { ref, computed } from 'vue';

const firstName = ref<string>('John');
const lastName = ref<string>('Doe');

const fullName = computed<string>(() => {
  return firstName.value + ' ' + lastName.value;
});
```

Benefits:

- Better readability.
- You can be more sure what the output of the system will be.

Composables and TypeScript: A Perfect Match

The Composition API and TypeScript work together beautifully to promote code reuse and maintainability. You can use composables to encapsulate reusable logic and then add type annotations to your composables to ensure type safety.

```
      // useMousePosition.ts
import { ref, onMounted, onUnmounted, Ref } from 'vue';

interface MousePosition {
  x: Ref<number>;
  y: Ref<number>;
}

export function useMousePosition(): MousePosition {
  const x = ref(0);
  const y = ref(0);

  const updateMousePosition = (event: MouseEvent) => {
    x.value = event.clientX;
    y.value = event.clientY;
  };

  onMounted(() => {
    window.addEventListener('mousemove',
updateMousePosition);
  });

  onUnmounted(() => {
    window.removeEventListener('mousemove',
updateMousePosition);
  });

  return {
    x,
    y
  };
}
```

In this example, we define a MousePosition interface that describes the structure of the object returned by the useMousePosition composable. We then use this interface as the return type annotation for the useMousePosition function.

Type Safety Across the Board: Props, Events, and More

TypeScript can be used to type your props, custom emitted values, and more, giving you a full system of checks and balances.

Practical Example: A Type-Safe To-Do List

Let's create a practical example of a type-safe to-do list using the Composition API and TypeScript:

```
    <template>
  <div>
    <h1>To-Do List</h1>
    <input type="text" v-model="newTodo"
@keyup.enter="addTodo" placeholder="Add a to-do...">
    <ul>
      <li v-for="todo in todos" :key="todo.id">{{ todo.text
}}</li>
    </ul>
  </div>
</template>

<script lang="ts">
import { ref, reactive, defineComponent } from 'vue';

interface Todo {
  id: number;
  text: string;
}

export default defineComponent({
  setup() {
    const newTodo = ref<string>('');
    const todos = reactive<Todo[]>([]);

    const addTodo = () => {
      if (newTodo.value.trim() !== '') {
        const todo: Todo = { id: Date.now(), text:
newTodo.value };
        todos.push(todo);
        newTodo.value = '';
      }
    };

    return {
      newTodo,
      todos,
      addTodo
    };
```

```
    }
});
</script>
```

- defineComponent: This helper function properly infers component prop types, and should be used whenever possible.

Personal Insight: TypeScript: Confidence in Code

Using TypeScript with Vue.js has given me a new level of confidence in my code. I know that the TypeScript compiler is watching my back, catching type errors and preventing runtime bugs. This allows me to focus on the logic of my application, rather than worrying about potential type-related issues.

Conclusion: The Synergy of Typing and Composability

The Composition API and TypeScript are a powerful combination that can significantly improve the quality, maintainability, and scalability of your Vue.js applications. This finishes the tutorial on advanced composition API. Congratulations on reaching the end.

Part 3: Building Modern Applications

Chapter 7: State Management with Pinia – Organizing Data for Large-Scale Applications

As your Vue.js applications grow beyond simple components, managing the application's state—the data that drives your UI—becomes increasingly complex. Passing data back and forth between components using props and events can quickly become unwieldy and difficult to maintain, especially when dealing with data that needs to be accessed and modified by multiple components across different parts of the application. This is where dedicated state management comes in.

In this chapter, we'll explore Pinia, the recommended state management library for Vue.js 3. We'll learn how to use Pinia to organize your application's state in a clear, consistent, and maintainable way. We are going to deep dive in State.

7.1 Introduction to State Management – Understanding the Need: When Components Aren't Enough

As you begin building Vue.js applications, you quickly learn to appreciate the component model. Breaking down your UI into reusable, self-contained pieces seems like a natural and efficient way to organize your code. And for small, simple applications, it often *is* enough.

However, as your applications grow in size and complexity, you'll inevitably encounter situations where components need to share data, interact with each other, and manage the application's overall state. Passing data directly between components using props and events—the standard Vue.js component communication mechanisms—can become cumbersome and difficult to maintain. You start seeing a problem: Data is too far away from related methods.

This is where state management comes in.

The Problem: Prop Drilling and Event Chaining – A Tangled Web

In a complex Vue.js application, data often needs to be shared between components that are not directly related. For example, you might have a user profile component that needs to access the user's authentication status, which is managed in a separate authentication component.

To share this data using props and events, you would have to pass the authentication status down through multiple levels of the component tree, even if the intermediate components don't actually need the data themselves. This is known as *prop drilling*.

Similarly, to update the authentication status, you would have to emit an event from the authentication component, which would then be passed up through multiple levels of the component tree until it reaches the component that actually manages the authentication state. This is known as *event chaining*.

Prop drilling and event chaining can make your code harder to read, understand, and maintain. It also makes it more difficult to refactor your code, as changes to one component can have ripple effects throughout the entire component tree.

Understanding State: The Key to Application Behavior

At its core, a "state" is any piece of data that is used to render your application and determine its behavior. It's the fundamental information that defines what your application displays and how it responds to user interactions.

The state can include a wide range of things:

- User authentication status
- User profile information
- Shopping cart contents
- Application settings
- Data fetched from an API
- UI state (e.g., whether a modal is open or closed)

Centralized State: A Single Source of Truth

State management is all about centralizing and organizing your application's state. Instead of scattering data across multiple components, you store it in a central *store* that acts as a single source of truth.

This central store provides a consistent and predictable way to access and modify the application's state. Components can subscribe to the store to receive updates whenever the state changes, and they can dispatch actions to modify the state in a controlled and predictable way.

The Solution: A Dedicated State Management System

State management systems address all of the mentioned issues. They provide a shared hub to move data across components with ease. By using a tool like Pinia, you can:

- Track user information across the entire app.
- Change UI parameters at the drop of a hat.
- React easily to new API updates.

Benefits of Centralized State Management

- **Single Source of Truth:** Centralizes your application's data in a single location, making it easier to understand and maintain.
- **Predictable State Mutations:** Provides a clear and consistent way to modify the application's state, preventing unexpected side effects.
- **Improved Testability:** Centralized state makes it easier to test your application's logic and behavior.
- **Enhanced Collaboration:** Makes it easier for multiple developers to work on the same application by providing a shared understanding of the application's data flow.
- **Better Performance:** State management libraries often use techniques like caching and dependency tracking to optimize performance and prevent unnecessary re-renders.

Personal Insight: A Before-and-After Story

I clearly recall working on a project where I initially dismissed the need for a state management system. I thought I could manage the application's data using props and events. However, as the project grew, the codebase became increasingly difficult to maintain, and I found myself spending more and more time debugging prop drilling and event chaining issues.

Finally, I decided to refactor the application using Vuex (this was before Pinia). The results were dramatic. The codebase became much cleaner and more organized, and I was able to refactor and add new features much more easily. It was a clear demonstration of the benefits of centralized state management.

Thinking Architecturally: State Management as a Design Pattern

State management is not just a library or a set of tools; it's a design pattern. It's a way of thinking about how to structure your application's data and how components interact with that data. By embracing the principles of state management, you can create more robust, maintainable, and scalable Vue.js applications.

A Word on Simplicity: When State Management Might Be Overkill

It's important to note that state management is not always necessary. For small, simple applications, the overhead of setting up and managing a state management system can outweigh the benefits.

If your application has only a few components and doesn't require complex data sharing, you might be better off sticking with props and events. However, as soon as your application starts to grow in size and complexity, it's time to consider adopting a state management system.

The Next Step: Pinia - A Modern State Management Solution

There are various state management libraries available for Vue.js, but Pinia has emerged as the recommended and most modern solution. We'll see how Pinia solves each of the data issues discussed so far.

7.2 Setting Up Pinia – Getting Started: Preparing Your Vue.js Application for Centralized State Management

Now that you understand the need for state management and the benefits of Pinia, it's time to get your hands dirty and set up Pinia in your Vue.js application. This section will guide you through the installation and configuration process, providing you with the foundation you need to start building powerful and scalable applications.

Think of this as preparing your workshop for a major project. You need to gather the right tools, organize your workspace, and make sure everything is ready before you can start building.

Prerequisites: A Clean Vue.js Project

Before you can install and configure Pinia, you'll need a Vue.js project. If you don't already have one, you can create a new project using the Vue CLI:

```
vue create my-pinia-project
```

During the project creation process, you can choose to include TypeScript, a CSS pre-processor, and other features. These choices will affect the structure of your project, but the basic steps for setting up Pinia will be the same.

Step 1: Installing the Pinia Package

The first step is to install the pinia package using npm or yarn:

```
npm install pinia
# OR
yarn add pinia
```

This command will download the Pinia library and add it to your project's node_modules directory.

Step 2: Creating a Pinia Instance

Once Pinia is installed, you need to create a Pinia instance in your application's entry point. This is typically the main.js or main.ts file in your project.

```
import { createApp } from 'vue';
import { createPinia } from 'pinia';
import App from './App.vue';

const pinia = createPinia(); // Create a Pinia instance
const app = createApp(App);

app.use(pinia); // Register Pinia as a plugin
app.mount('#app');
```

Explanation:

- import { createPinia } from 'pinia';: This imports the createPinia function from the pinia package.
- const pinia = createPinia();: This creates a new Pinia instance.
- app.use(pinia);: This registers Pinia as a plugin with your Vue application. This makes Pinia's features available to all components in your application.

The createPinia() Function: Setting the Stage for State Management

The createPinia() function is what sets the stage for state management in your Vue.js application. It creates a new Pinia instance, which acts as the central hub for all your stores.

By registering Pinia as a plugin with your Vue application, you make the Pinia instance available to all components in your application through the $pinia property. However, it's generally recommended to use the useStore function (which we'll discuss in the next section) to access stores in your components, as this provides better type safety and encapsulation.

Optional: Root Store Injection (Not Recommended):

In Vue 2, it was common to inject the store instance into the root component using the provide option. This is no longer necessary in Vue 3 with Pinia, as Pinia automatically makes the store instance available to all components.

TypeScript Considerations: Type Safety from the Start

If you're using TypeScript, you can add type annotations to your Pinia instance and to your stores to ensure type safety throughout your application.

```
      import { createApp } from 'vue';
import { createPinia, Pinia } from 'pinia';
import App from './App.vue';

const pinia: Pinia = createPinia(); // Create a Pinia
instance
const app = createApp(App);

app.use(pinia); // Register Pinia as a plugin
app.mount('#app');
```

By adding the : Pinia type annotation to the pinia variable, you tell TypeScript that this variable should hold a Pinia instance. This allows TypeScript to catch any type errors related to the Pinia instance early on.

Verifying Your Setup: A Quick Test

To verify that Pinia has been set up correctly, you can add a simple test to your App.vue component:

```
      <template>
  <div>
    <h1>Welcome to My App</h1>
    <p>Pinia is running!</p>
  </div>
</template>

<script>
export default {
  mounted() {
    console.log('Pinia is available:', this.$pinia);
  }
};
</script>
```

If you see "Pinia is available: [object Object]" in the console, it means that Pinia has been successfully set up in your application.

A Word on Project Structure:

While this section focuses on setting up Pinia, it's also important to think about how you'll structure your stores within your project. A common approach is to create a stores directory in the root of your project and place each store in its own file.

Personal Insight: Smooth Sailing with Pinia's Setup

Setting up Pinia is a breeze compared to some other state management solutions I've used in the past. The installation process is straightforward, and the API is intuitive and easy to learn. I was able to get up and running with Pinia in a matter of minutes, which allowed me to focus on building my application rather than wrestling with configuration.

Conclusion: Ready to Manage State Like a Pro

You've now successfully set up Pinia in your Vue.js application. This provides the foundation for managing your data well. The next step, is to define them and show how to call them.

With Pinia installed and configured, you're ready to start defining stores and managing your application's state in a clear, consistent, and maintainable way. You've laid the groundwork for building scalable and robust Vue.js applications that are easy to understand, test, and maintain. Now let's dig in.

7.3 Defining Stores: State, Getters, and Actions – Structuring Your Data: The Blueprint for State Management

With Pinia installed and configured, it's time to learn how to define stores. As mentioned earlier, a store is a container that holds your application's state and provides methods for accessing and modifying that state. It's the blueprint for how your data will be managed. Defining your stores well is vital for the rest of your application's code, so let's go.

Think of a store as a well-organized toolbox. It contains all the tools you need to work with a specific set of data, such as data properties, computed properties, and methods for modifying the data.

The Core Components: State, Getters, and Actions

A Pinia store consists of three key parts:

- **State:** The reactive data that represents the application's state. This is where you store the data that your components will use.
- **Getters:** Functions that derive data from the state. These are similar to computed properties in Vue.js components.
- **Actions:** Methods that modify the state. These are the *only* way to modify the state directly. Actions can be synchronous or asynchronous.

Defining a Store: The defineStore Function

To define a store, you use the defineStore function from Pinia. The defineStore function takes two arguments:

1. **The store ID:** A unique identifier for the store. This is used to connect the store to the Pinia devtools and to identify the store when using dependency injection. It is recommended to name each store individually.
2. **A configuration object:** An object that contains the state, getters, and actions for the store.

```
import { defineStore } from 'pinia';

export const useCounterStore = defineStore('counter', {
```

```
  state: () => ({
    count: 0,
    name: 'John Doe'
  }),
  getters: {
    doubleCount: (state) => state.count * 2,
    greeting: (state) => `Hello, ${state.name}!`,
  },
  actions: {
    increment() {
      this.count++;
    },
    decrement() {
      this.count--;
    },
    setName(newName) {
      this.name = newName;
    }
  }
});
```

Delving Deeper: Unpacking the Configuration Object

Let's take a closer look at the configuration object and its key properties:

- **state:** The state option is a function that returns an object containing the reactive data properties. This function is used so that each component has its own copy of the data when used.

```
    state: () => ({
  count: 0,
  name: 'John Doe'
})
```

- **getters:** The getters option is an object that defines the store's getters. Each getter is a function that takes the state as an argument and returns a derived value.

```
    getters: {
  doubleCount: (state) => state.count * 2,
  greeting: (state) => `Hello, ${state.name}!`
}
```

Note: You can use other getters in a getter!

- **actions:** The actions option is an object that defines the store's actions. Each action is a method that modifies the state. Actions can be synchronous or asynchronous.

```
    actions: {
  increment() {
    this.count++;
  },
  decrement() {
    this.count--;
  },
  async setName(newName) {
    // Simulate an asynchronous operation
    await new Promise(resolve => setTimeout(resolve, 500));
    this.name = newName;
  }
}
```

Key Notes:
1. **Accessing the State:** Within actions, you can access the store's state using this. However, TypeScript requires special handling.
2. **Action Payloads:** Actions should accept a payload argument containing any data needed to perform the state mutation.
3. **Asynchronous Actions:** Actions can be asynchronous, allowing you to perform tasks such as making API calls or interacting with a database.

"reset" Store State (Helpful Action Example):
A helpful pattern for testing is to also add a reset method that copies the value of the initial state to the current one:

```
    actions: {
  reset() {
    Object.assign(this, initialState())
  },
}
```

Why No Mutations? The Simplification of State Management

Unlike Vuex, Pinia *does not* use mutations. Mutations are synchronous functions that are used to modify the state in Vuex. The Pinia team decided to remove mutations in favor of actions, as they felt that mutations added unnecessary complexity and boilerplate to the state management process.

By only allowing state to be modified through actions, Pinia provides a more predictable and consistent way to manage your application's state.

TypeScript Considerations: Adding Type Safety

If you're using TypeScript, you can add type annotations to your store to ensure type safety:

```
    import { defineStore } from 'pinia';

interface CounterState {
  count: number;
  name: string;
}

export const useCounterStore = defineStore('counter', {
  state: (): CounterState => ({
    count: 0,
    name: 'John Doe'
  }),
  getters: {
    doubleCount: (state: CounterState) => state.count * 2,
    greeting: (state: CounterState) => `Hello,
${state.name}!`
  },
  actions: {
    increment() {
      this.count++;
    },
    decrement() {
      this.count--;
    },
    setName(newName: string) {
      this.name = newName;
    }
  }
});
```

Key Points:

- We define a CounterState interface that describes the structure of the store's state.
- We use the CounterState interface as a type annotation for the state function, the getter functions, and the action parameters.

Personal Insight: From Confusion to Clarity

I initially struggled to understand the purpose of stores in Vuex. They seemed like an overly complex way to manage data. However, once I started using Pinia, I realized the value of having a centralized and predictable way to manage my application's state. Pinia's simpler API and the elimination of mutations made state management much more intuitive and enjoyable.

Conclusion: A Solid Foundation for Scalable Applications

Defining well-structured stores with clear state, getters, and actions is essential for building scalable and maintainable Vue.js applications. By following the principles and techniques outlined in this section, you can create a state management system that is easy to understand, test, and extend. Then let's use that structure in a component.

7.4 Using Stores in Components – Connecting Data to the UI: Bridging the Gap Between State Management and the User Interface

You've defined your stores, complete with their state, getters, and actions. Now, the crucial step: connecting those stores to your Vue.js components and making the data accessible in your UI. This section demonstrates how to seamlessly integrate Pinia stores into your components, enabling them to react to changes, display data, and trigger actions that modify the application's state.

Think of this as establishing a communication channel between your application's data By convention this is use[StoreName]Store.

```
import { useCounterStore } from './stores/counter';
```

Then, you can call the useCounterStore function within the setup() function to get access to an instance of the store:

```
    <template>
  <div>
    <p>Count: {{ count }}</p>
    <p>Double Count: {{ doubleCount }}</p>
    <button @click="increment">Increment</button>
    <button @click="decrement">Decrement</button>
  </div>
</template>
```

```
<script>
import { useCounterStore } from './stores/counter';

export default {
  setup() {
    const counter = useCounterStore(); // Get the store
instance

    return {
      count: counter.count, // Access the state
      doubleCount: counter.doubleCount, // Access the getter
      increment: counter.increment, // Access the action
      decrement: counter.decrement // Access the action
    };
  }
};
</script>
```

Explanation:

- const counter = useCounterStore();: Calls the useCounterStore function to get an instance of the store. This instance provides access to the store's state, getters, and actions.

Mapping State, Getters, and Actions: Explicitly Exposing Data

In the above example, we explicitly map the store's state, getters, and actions to local variables in the setup() function. This approach provides better readability and makes it clear which data properties and methods are being used in the template.

```
    return {
  count: counter.count, // Access the state
  doubleCount: counter.doubleCount, // Access the getter
  increment: counter.increment, // Access the action
  decrement: counter.decrement // Access the action
};
```

By explicitly mapping the store's properties to local variables, you make it easier to understand which data properties are being used in the template and to avoid naming conflicts.

**Shorthand: Direct Store Access (Caveats and its visual representation. Your components will become reactive listeners, automatically updating whenever the data in the store changes.

Accessing the Store: The useStore Hook

To use a store in a component, you first need to import the useStore function that you defined in the previous section. Then, you can call the useStore function within the setup() function to get access to the store's state, getters, and actions.

Let's work with an example, and show how to use the data defined in the following component:

```
      // stores/counter.js
import { defineStore } from 'pinia';

export const useCounterStore = defineStore('counter', {
  state: () => ({
    count: 0,
    name: 'John Doe'
  }),
  getters: {
    doubleCount: (state) => state.count * 2,
    greeting: (state) => `Hello, ${state.name}!`
  },
  actions: {
    increment() {
      this.count++;
    },
    decrement() {
      this. Apply!)**
```

```
You can also access the store's state, getters, and actions
directly in the template without mapping them to local
variables.

```html
<template>
  <div>
    <p>Count: {{ counter.count }}</p>
    <p>Double Count: {{ counter.doubleCount }}</p>
    <button @click="counter.increment">Increment</button>
    <button @click="counter.decrement">Decrement</button>
  </div>
</template>

      import { useCounterStore } from './stores/counter';
```
```

```
export default {
  setup() {
    const counter = useCounterStore(); // Get the store
instance

    return {
      counter // Expose the entire store
    };
  }
};
```

This approach is more concise, but it can make your template harder to read and understand. It's generally recommended to explicitly map the state, getters, and actions to local variables, especially for complex components. Also this will remove the easy access of code completion.

The Best of Both Worlds: storeToRefs

In Pinia, storeToRefs provides a handy utility to destructure a store while maintaining reactivity:

```
      import { useCounterStore } from './stores/counter'
import { storeToRefs } from 'pinia'

export default {
  setup() {
    const counter = useCounterStore()

    // `count` and `doubleCount` are now refs
    // will uncount--;
    },
    setName(newName) {
      this.name = newName;
    }
  }
});

      <template>
  <div>
    <p>Count: {{ count }}</p>
    <p>Double Count: {{ doubleCount }}</p>
    <p>Greeting: {{ greeting }}</p>
    <button @click="increment">Increment</button>
    <button @click="decrement">Decrement</button>
    <button @click="setName('Jane Doe')">Change Name</button>
  </div>
</template>
```

```
<script>
import { useCounterStore } from './stores/counter';

export default {
  setup() {
    const counter = useCounterStore(); // Get the store
instance

    return {
      count: counter.count, // Map the state to a local
variable
      doubleCount: counter.doubleCount, // Map the getter to
a local variable
      greeting: counter.greeting, // Map the getter to a
local variable
      increment: counter.increment, // Map the action to a
local variable
      decrement: counter.decrement, // Map the action to a
local variable
      setName: counter.setName // Map the action to a local
variable
    };
  }
};
</script>
```

Explanation:

1. **Import the Store:** import { useCounterStore } from './stores/counter'; imports the useCounterStore function from the stores/counter.js file.
2. **Get the Store Instance:** const counter = useCounterStore(); calls the useCounterStore function to get an instance of the store. This instance provides access to the store's state, getters, and actions.
   3.wrap the refs automatically
   const { count, doubleCount } = storeToRefs(counter)

   return {
   count,
   doubleCount,
   increment: counter.increment,
   decrement: counter.decrement,
   }
   },
   }

Actions Still Need Accessing:

A caveat is that the `actions` are *not* refs, and therefore, you will still need to access actions through `counter.actionName`. This helps in the maintainability of the system.

Why Use storeToRefs?

With `storeToRefs`, you maintain a clean division of the code and you don't lose out on TypeScript type hinting in your stores.

Modifying the State: Dispatching Actions

To modify the state, you call one of the store's actions. Actions are methods that are defined in the store's configuration object. In the store to refs example above, actions are called via `counter.increment` or similar.

Practical Example: A Shopping Cart Component

Let's create a practical example of a shopping cart component that uses a Pinia store to manage the cart items:

```vue
<template>
  <div>
    <h2>Shopping Cart</h2>
    <ul>
      <li v-for="item in cartItems" :key="item.id">
        {{ item.name }} - ${{ item.price }} - Quantity: {{
item.quantity }}
        <button
@click="removeFromCart(item.id)">Remove</button>
```

Map the State, Getters, and Actions: We then map the store's state, getters, and actions to local variables in the `setup()` function so that they can be used in the template. This is important for maintaining reactivity.

Accessing State Directly: The `storeToRefs` Helper (Recommended)

As you can see from the previous example, it can be tedious to manually map each state property, getter, and action to local variables. Pinia provides a helper function called `storeToRefs` that simplifies this process.

The `storeToRefs` function takes a store instance as an argument and returns an object containing refs for all of the store's state properties. This allows you to destructure the object and access the state properties directly in your template without losing reactivity.

```vue
<template>
  <div>
    <p>Count: {{ count }}</p>
    <p>Double Count: {{ doubleCount }}</p>
    <p>Greeting: {{ greeting }}</p>
    <button @click="increment">Increment</button>
    <button @click="decrement">Decrement</button>
    <button @click="setName('Jane Doe')">Change Name</button>
  </div>
</template>

<script>
import { useCounterStore } from './stores/counter';
import { storeToRefs } from 'pinia';

export default {
  setup() {
    const counter = useCounterStore();

    const { count, doubleCount, greeting</li>
    </ul>
    <h3>Total: ${{ cartTotal }}</h3>
  </div>
</template>

<script>
import { useCartStore } from './stores/cart';
import { storeToRefs } from 'pinia'

export default {
  setup() {
    const cart = useCartStore();
    const {cartTotal, cartItems} = storeToRefs(cart);

    const removeFromCart = (itemId) => {
      cart.removeFromCart(itemId);
    };

    return {
      cartItems,
      cartTotal,
      removeFromCart
    };
  }
};
</script>
```

```
// stores/cart.js
import { defineStore } from 'pinia';

export const useCartStore = defineStore('cart', {
  state: () => ({
    items: [
      { id: 1, name: 'Product A', price: 10, quantity: 2 },
      { id: 2, name: 'Product B', price: 20, quantity: 1 }
    ]
  }),
  getters: {
    cartTotal: (state) => {
      return state.items.reduce((total, item) => {
        return total + item.price * item.quantity;
      }, 0);
    }
  },
  actions: {
    removeFromCart(itemId) {
      this.items = this.items.filter(item => item.id !==
itemId);
    }
  }
});
```

In this example, the useCartStore function returns an instance of the cart store. The component then accesses the cartTotal getter to display the total value of the cart, and it calls the removeFromCart action to remove an item from the cart.

TypeScript Considerations: Maintaining Type Safety

If you're using TypeScript, you can add type annotations to your component's setup() function to ensure type safety when accessing and modifying the store's data:

Personal Insight: Putting it All Together: A Sense of Empowerment

Connecting my Vue.js components to Pinia stores has given me a new sense of empowerment. I can now manage my application's state with confidence, knowing that my data is organized, predictable, and easy to access and modify. The dev tools also make it easier than ever to visualize.

Conclusion: From State to UI with Ease

Connecting your Vue.js components to Pinia stores is essential for building scalable and maintainable applications. By understanding how to access the store, use its getters, and dispatch actions, you can create user interfaces that are responsive to changes in your application's state and that provide a seamless user experience. We have now covered everything about one specific store, in the next section we will show how they can easily be organized.

7.5 Organizing Stores with Modules – Scaling Your Data Structure: From a Single Toolbox to a Well-Organized Workshop

As your Vue.js applications grow in size and complexity, the single-store approach can quickly become unwieldy. Imagine trying to manage the state for an e-commerce application with a single store that contains everything from user authentication to product listings to shopping cart details. It would be a nightmare to navigate and maintain!

That's why as we said before, Pinia encourages you to break down your stores into smaller and easily maintained chunks by building multiple smaller stores, that are composed together, making the whole a manageable project!

This architecture is different than Vuex which has a more formal approach. The design of Pinia is made for simpler data, that is easily broken down, which has become more commonly used.

The Problem with a Single Store: Maintainability and Scalability Challenges

- **Complexity:** A single store can become overwhelming as your application grows, making it harder to understand and maintain the code.
- **Naming Conflicts:** As more developers contribute to the project, the risk of naming conflicts increases.
- **Testability:** It can be difficult to test a large, monolithic store in isolation.

The Solution: Modular Stores – Dividing and Conquering Complexity

The secret to success isn't working harder, it's working smarter. So what do composable stores offer?

- **Separation of Concerns:** Focuses your store to individual specific tasks.
- **Increased clarity:** Better for reasoning about and troubleshooting state
- **Simpler Tests:** Since each store has its own state and functions, testing is simpler.

Creating Multiple Stores: Breaking Down the Monolith

Instead of defining a single large store, you can create multiple smaller stores that each manage a specific part of your application's state. For example, you might have a user store for managing user authentication and profile information, a products store for managing product listings, and a cart store for managing the shopping cart.

To create multiple stores, you simply define multiple functions that call defineStore, each with a unique store ID:

```
      // stores/user.js
import { defineStore } from 'pinia';

export const useUserStore = defineStore('user', {
  state: () => ({
    name: 'John Doe',
    email: 'john.doe@example.com'
  }),
  // ...
});

// stores/cart.js
import { defineStore } from 'pinia';

export const useCartStore = defineStore('cart', {
  state: () => ({
    items: []
  }),
  // ...
});
```

In this example, we've created two stores: useUserStore and useCartStore. Each store manages a specific part of the application's state.

Using Multiple Stores in Components: Bringing It All Together

To use multiple stores in a component, you simply import the corresponding useStore functions and call them within the setup() function:

```
    <template>
  <div>
    <h2>User Profile</h2>
    <p>Name: {{ user.name }}</p>
    <p>Email: {{ user.email }}</p>

    <h2>Shopping Cart</h2>
    <ul>
      <li v-for="item in cart.items" :key="item.id">{{
item.name }}</li>
    </ul>
  </div>
</template>

<script>
import { useUserStore } from './stores/user';
import { useCartStore } from './stores/cart';
import { storeToRefs } from 'pinia'

export default {
  setup() {
    const user = useUserStore();
    const cart = useCartStore();

    const {items} = storeToRefs(cart);

    return {
      user,
      cartItems: items
    };
  }
};
</script>
```

In this example, the component uses both the useUserStore and useCartStore to access the user profile and shopping cart data.

Example: Sharing Data using Multiple Stores:
If you have code that needs to share data, composables can help.

```
    <template>
  <div>
```

```
    <h2>Cart Summary</h2>
    <p>Number of Items: {{ cartCount }}</p>
    <p>Total is greater than zero? {{ greaterThanZero }}</p>
  </div>
</template>

<script>
import { useCartStore } from './stores/cart';
import { computed } from 'vue';

export default {
  setup() {
    const cart = useCartStore();

    const cartCount = computed(() => {
      return cart.items.length
    });

    const greaterThanZero = computed(() => {
      return cartCount.value > 0
    });

    return {
      cartCount,
      greaterThanZero,
    };
  }
};
</script>
```

TypeScript Considerations: Enforcing Type Safety Across Stores

If you're using TypeScript, you can add type annotations to your stores and components to ensure type safety across your entire application.

Personal Insight: The Freedom of Modularity

Modular stores have given me the freedom to structure my Vue.js applications in a way that makes sense for the specific domain I'm working in. I no longer feel constrained by the limitations of a single store.

Conclusion: Organize for Success

Organizing your stores into modules is essential for building scalable and maintainable Vue.js applications. By following the principles and techniques outlined in this section, you can create a state management system that is easy to understand, test, and extend. With a scalable application, the possibilities of your future are endless. This concludes the state management section, now we can move on to routing.

Chapter 8: Routing with Vue Router – Navigating Your Single-Page Application

While Vue.js excels at building reusable UI components, it's equally important to consider how users will navigate between different parts of your application. This is where routing comes into play. In this chapter, we'll explore Vue Router, the official routing library for Vue.js. We'll learn how to use Vue Router to create a seamless and intuitive navigation experience in your single-page applications (SPAs).

Think of Vue Router as the roadmap for your application. It defines the different routes (URLs) that your application supports, and it maps those routes to the corresponding components that should be rendered. It also provides a way to navigate between routes programmatically and to protect certain routes from unauthorized access.

8.1 Introduction to Vue Router – From Static Pages to Dynamic Navigation: Embracing the SPA Paradigm

For years, the traditional way to build websites involved creating separate HTML pages for each section of content. When a user clicked a link, the browser would make a new request to the server, download the new HTML page, and completely reload the page. This approach, while simple, resulted in a clunky user experience with noticeable delays and page flickers.

With the rise of JavaScript frameworks like Vue.js, a new paradigm emerged: the single-page application (SPA). In an SPA, the entire application is loaded into a single HTML page, and the framework handles all subsequent navigation and content updates dynamically, without requiring the browser to reload the page. This results in a much faster, smoother, and more responsive user experience.

That speed comes with a challenge. With the movement to SPAs, a new concept is added to your website: Routing.

This Section will dig into:

- What Vue Router does to address this concept.
- What Vue Router does to help create a great product for the customer.

The Evolution: From Server-Side Rendering to Client-Side Routing

Before SPAs became popular, web applications relied heavily on *server-side rendering*. This meant that the server was responsible for generating the HTML for each page and sending it to the browser. While this approach had some advantages (such as better SEO), it also had several drawbacks:

- **Slow Page Loads:** Each page request required a round trip to the server, resulting in noticeable delays.
- **Full Page Reloads:** The entire page had to be reloaded every time the user navigated to a new page, leading to a jarring user experience.
- **Limited Interactivity:** The level of interactivity was limited by the need to communicate with the server for every action.

SPAs address these limitations by performing most of the rendering and logic on the client-side (in the browser). This allows for faster page loads, smoother transitions, and a more interactive user experience.

The Birth of Routing: Mapping URLs to Components

In a single-page application, the URL still plays an important role. It allows users to bookmark specific sections of the application, share links with others, and use the browser's back and forward buttons to navigate between different states.

However, in an SPA, the URL is no longer directly tied to a physical HTML file on the server. Instead, it's managed by a *routing library* like Vue Router.

Vue Router is responsible for:

- **Mapping URLs to Components:** Defining which component should be rendered for each URL in the application. This allows you to create a logical structure for your application and to display different content based on the URL.
- **Managing Browser History:** Keeping track of the user's navigation history and allowing them to use the back and forward buttons to navigate between routes.
- **Updating the URL:** Updating the URL in the browser's address bar when the user navigates to a new route.

Why Vue Router?

- **Seamless SPA Experience:** Enables you to build single-page applications with a seamless and responsive user experience.
- **Declarative Routing:** Provides a declarative way to define your application's routes and their corresponding components, by telling which route to look for.
- **Dynamic Route Matching:** Supports dynamic route matching, allowing you to create routes with parameters that can be used to display different content based on the URL.
- **Navigation Guards:** Provides navigation guards that allow you to protect certain routes from unauthorized access or to perform other actions before or after a route is activated.
- **History Management:** Manages the browser's history, allowing users to use the back and forward buttons to navigate between routes in a good way.
- **Lazy Loading:** Supports lazy loading of components, allowing you to improve the initial load time of your application.

The Core Concept: Mapping Routes to Components

At its heart, Vue Router is all about mapping routes to components. A *route* is simply a URL path that you want to associate with a specific component. When the user navigates to a particular route, Vue Router will render the corresponding component in the browser.

Let's consider a simple example:

```
    const routes = [
  { path: '/', component: Home },
  { path: '/about', component: About }
];
```

In this example, we're defining two routes:

- The / route is associated with the Home component.
- The /about route is associated with the About component.

When the user navigates to the / URL, Vue Router will render the Home component. When the user navigates to the /about URL, Vue Router will render the About component.

Personal Insight: From Confusion to Clarity

When I first started working with Vue.js, I found the concept of routing a bit confusing. I was used to building websites with separate HTML pages, and the idea of managing everything within a single page seemed strange.

However, once I started using Vue Router, I quickly realized its power and flexibility. It allowed me to create a much more dynamic and responsive user experience, and it made it easier to organize and maintain my code.

A Word on Flexibility: More Than Just URLs

While URLs are the most common way to trigger route changes, Vue Router can also be used to respond to other events, such as form submissions or button clicks. This allows you to create a truly interactive and dynamic user experience.

Conclusion: Embracing the Power of Routing

Routing is a fundamental concept in modern web development, and Vue Router provides a powerful and flexible way to manage routing in your Vue.js applications. By understanding the principles of routing and the features of Vue Router, you can create single-page applications that are fast, responsive, and easy to navigate. Let's see how to start routing with Vue Router.

8.2 Setting Up Vue Router – Preparing Your Application for Navigation: Laying the Foundation for Seamless Transitions

You now understand the principles of routing and the role of Vue Router in single-page applications. It’s time to get practical and prepare your Vue.js application for navigation. This section will walk you through the steps of installing Vue Router, creating a router instance, and integrating it into your application.

Think of setting up Vue Router as laying the foundation for a building. A solid foundation is essential for ensuring the stability and longevity of the structure. Similarly, a properly configured Vue Router is essential for creating a smooth and maintainable navigation experience in your Vue.js application.

Step 1: Installing the vue-router Package

The first step is to install the vue-router package using npm or yarn:

```
npm install vue-router@4
# OR
yarn add vue-router@4
```

Important Note: The @4 is crucial. Vue Router 3 is designed for Vue 2, and we want to use Vue Router 4, which is compatible with Vue 3.

This command will download the Vue Router library and add it to your project's node_modules directory.

Step 2: Creating a Router Instance – Defining Your Application's Map

Once Vue Router is installed, you need to create a router instance in your application. A common practice is to create a dedicated directory called router and add an index.js (or index.ts if you're using TypeScript) file inside it. This file will contain the code for creating and configuring the router.

Here's an example of how to create a router instance:

```
// router/index.js
import { createRouter, createWebHistory } from 'vue-router';
import Home from '../components/Home.vue';
import About from '../components/About.vue';

const routes = [
  { path: '/', name: 'Home', component: Home },
  { path: '/about', name: 'About', component: About }
];

const router = createRouter({
  history: createWebHistory(),
  routes
});

export default router;
```

Understanding the Code:

- **import { createRouter, createWebHistory } from 'vue-router';:** This imports the necessary functions from the vue-router package.
    - createRouter: This function is used to create a router instance.
    - createWebHistory: This function is used to create a history object that uses the browser's history API. This is the recommended history mode for most applications.
- **import Home from '../components/Home.vue'; and import About from '../components/About.vue';:** These import the components that you want to associate with your routes. Make sure the paths are correct.
- **const routes = [...];:** This defines an array of route objects. Each route object has the following properties:
    - path: The URL path for the route (e.g., /, /about).
    - name: A unique name for the route. This is optional, but it's recommended as a best practice to help with programmatic navigation and create readable code.
    - component: The component that should be rendered when the route is activated.
- **const router = createRouter({ ... });:** This creates a new router instance with the specified configuration.
    - history: createWebHistory(): Specifies that the router should use the browser's history API for navigation. This provides clean URLs without hash fragments.
    - routes: Specifies the array of route objects that define your application's routes.
- **export default router;:** This exports the router instance so that it can be imported and used in your main application.

History Modes: Choosing the Right Approach

Vue Router offers several history modes that determine how the router interacts with the browser's history:

- **createWebHistory():** This is the recommended history mode for most applications. It uses the browser's history API to provide clean URLs without hash fragments. However, it requires server-side configuration to ensure that all routes are properly handled.
- **createWebHashHistory():** This history mode uses the hash fragment (#) in the URL to simulate navigation. It doesn't require any server-side configuration, but it results in URLs that are less readable and less SEO-friendly.

- **createMemoryHistory():** This history mode doesn't interact with the browser's history at all. It's primarily used for testing and server-side rendering.

Step 3: Registering the Router with the Application – Making It Accessible

Once you've created a router instance, you need to register it as a plugin with your Vue application. This makes the router available to all components in your application.

To register the router, import the router instance in your main.js or main.ts file and call the app.use() method:

```
import { createApp } from 'vue';
import App from './App.vue';
import router from './router'; // Import the router

const app = createApp(App);

app.use(router); // Register the router
app.mount('#app');
```

Key Point: The order of the app.use() calls matters. Make sure you register the router *before* mounting the application.

Verifying Your Setup: A Quick Test

To verify that Vue Router has been set up correctly, you can add a simple test to your App.vue component:

```
<template>
  <div>
    <h1>My App</h1>
    <router-view></router-view>
  </div>
</template>
```

Create the Home and About components:

```
//components/Home.vue
<template>
    <h2>Home</h2>
```

```
</template>

      //components/About.vue
<template>
    <h2>About</h2>
</template>
```

If you see the content of the Home component displayed when you navigate to the / URL and the content of the About component displayed when you navigate to the /about URL, it means that Vue Router has been successfully set up in your application.

Personal Insight: The Power of Declarative Routing

One of the things I appreciate most about Vue Router is its declarative nature. I can simply define my application's routes in a configuration object, and Vue Router takes care of the rest. This makes my code more readable and easier to maintain.

Conclusion: Ready for Navigation

You've now successfully set up Vue Router in your Vue.js application. The framework has been laid for the rest of the application. Let's go.

8.3 Defining Routes and Navigation – Creating Your Application's Map: Charting the Course for Your Users

With Vue Router installed and configured, it's time to start defining your application's routes and creating navigation links. This section focuses on turning that app into something that users can interact with and enjoy. We're going to learn how you can link that Vue Router has set up with the rest of the UI. Defining the routes in Vue is like drawing a map of where different parts of the website exists.

Think of defining routes as drawing a map of your application's landscape. Each route represents a specific location in your application, and the navigation links act as roads that allow users to travel between these locations.

Defining Routes: Mapping URLs to Components

As you now know, routes are defined as an array of objects in your router configuration file (e.g., router/index.js or router/index.ts). Each route object represents a single route in your application and specifies the URL path, component, and other options for that route.

Each route object typically has the following properties:

- **path:** The URL path for the route (e.g., /, /about, /users/:id). This is the address that will appear in the browser's address bar.
- **name:** A unique name for the route. This is optional, but strongly recommended as it provides a convenient way to refer to the route in your code, and makes the code more readable. Also, using a name enables more programmatic features.
- **component:** The component that should be rendered when the route is activated. This is the component that will be displayed when the user navigates to the route.

Let's look at some examples:

```
const routes = [
  { path: '/', name: 'Home', component: Home },
  { path: '/about', name: 'About', component: About },
  { path: '/contact', name: 'Contact', component: Contact }
];
```

In this example, we're defining three routes:

- The / route is associated with the Home component and has the name Home.
- The /about route is associated with the About component and has the name About.
- The /contact route is associated with the Contact component and has the name Contact.

Creating Navigation Links: Guiding Your Users Through the App

To allow users to navigate between your application's routes, you need to create navigation links. Vue Router provides the <router-link> component for creating these links.

The <router-link> component is a special component that renders a link to a specific route. When the user clicks on the link, Vue Router will automatically update the component being displayed without reloading the page.

```
<router-link to="/">Home</router-link>
<router-link to="/about">About</router-link>
<router-link to="/contact">Contact</router-link>
```

This code will render three links that navigate to the /, /about, and /contact routes, respectively.

Using Route Names: A More Robust Approach

Instead of using the path property directly, it's often a better practice to use the name property to specify the target route. This makes your code more robust, as it decouples the navigation links from the actual URL paths. If you change the URL path for a route, you don't have to update all the navigation links that point to that route.

To use the name property, you need to pass an object to the to property of the <router-link> component:

```
<router-link :to="{ name: 'Home' }">Home</router-link>
<router-link :to="{ name: 'About' }">About</router-link>
<router-link :to="{ name: 'Contact' }">Contact</router-link>
```

In this example, we're using the name property to specify the target route for each navigation link. This approach is more robust and easier to maintain than using the path property directly.

Programmatic Navigation: Taking Control of the Flow

In addition to using the <router-link> component, you can also navigate between routes programmatically using the router.push() method. This is useful when you need to perform navigation based on a specific condition or user action. For this example we need to have set up the router to inject.

```
import { useRouter } from 'vue-router';

export default {
  setup() {
    const router = useRouter();
```

```
    const goToAbout = () => {
      router.push('/about'); // Navigate to the /about route
using path
    };

    const goToContact = () => {
      router.push({ name: 'Contact' }); // Navigate to the
Contact route using name
    };

    return {
      goToAbout,
      goToContact
    };
  },
  template: `
    <div>
      <button @click="goToAbout">Go to About</button>
      <button @click="goToContact">Go to Contact</button>
    </div>
  `
};
```

In this example, we're using the router.push() method to navigate to the /about and Contact routes when the corresponding buttons are clicked.

Practical Tips: The Path to Success

- **Use Descriptive Route Names:** Choose descriptive and meaningful names for your routes. This will make your code easier to understand and maintain.
- **Centralize Your Route Definitions:** Keep all of your route definitions in a single file (e.g., router/index.js or router/index.ts). This will make it easier to manage your application's routing configuration.
- **Use the <router-link> Component for Navigation:** Use the <router-link> component whenever possible for creating navigation links. This will ensure that your application provides a consistent and accessible navigation experience.

Personal Insight: Routing: The Backbone of SPAs

Mastering routing is essential for building successful single-page applications with Vue.js. It allows you to create a seamless and intuitive navigation experience that keeps your users engaged and helps them find the information they need.

Conclusion: Charting Your Application's Course

Defining routes and creating navigation links are fundamental steps in building a Vue.js application with Vue Router. By understanding how to use the <router-link> component, how to use route names, and how to navigate programmatically, you can create a navigation experience that is both user-friendly and maintainable. Now let's see how to do something more fun, like add parameters.

8.4 Route Parameters and Query Parameters – Creating Dynamic Routes: Adding Flexibility and Power to Your Navigation

In the previous section, we learned how to define basic routes and create navigation links in Vue Router. Now, let's take our routing skills to the next level by exploring route parameters and query parameters. These features allow you to create dynamic routes that can display different content based on the URL, making your application more flexible and powerful.

Think of route parameters and query parameters as variables that you can pass in the URL to customize the behavior of a specific route. They allow you to create dynamic user interfaces that adapt to different inputs and scenarios.

Route Parameters: Capturing Dynamic Segments in the URL

Route parameters are dynamic segments of the URL that are captured and passed to the component as props. They are defined using a colon (:) followed by the parameter name in the route path.

```
      const routes = [
  { path: '/users/:id', name: 'User', component: User },
  { path: '/products/:category/:productId', name: 'Product',
component: Product }
];
```

In this example, we're defining two routes with route parameters:

- The /users/:id route has a single route parameter called id.
- The /products/:category/:productId route has two route parameters: category and productId.

When the user navigates to a URL that matches one of these routes, Vue Router will extract the values of the route parameters from the URL and pass them to the corresponding component as props.

Accessing Route Parameters: The useRoute Composable

To access the route parameters in the component, you use the useRoute composable from Vue Router. The useRoute composable returns the current route object, which contains information about the route, including the route parameters.

```
    import { useRoute } from 'vue-router';

export default {
  setup() {
    const route = useRoute();
    const userId = route.params.id; // Access the id
parameter
    //Alternatively with Typescript:
    //const userId = route.params.id as string;

    return {
      userId
    };
  },
  template: `
    <div>
      <h2>User ID: {{ userId }}</h2>
    </div>
  `
};
```

Important Notes:

- **Type Safety:** If you're using TypeScript, you should add type annotations to your route parameters to ensure type safety.
- **Parameter Names:** Choose descriptive and meaningful names for your route parameters. This will make your code easier to understand and maintain.

Query Parameters: Passing Optional Data in the URL

Query parameters are optional data that is passed in the URL after a question mark (?). They are typically used to pass filter criteria, sorting options, or other non-essential data.

```
/products?category=electronics&sort=price&page=2
```

In this example, we're passing three query parameters:

- category: Specifies the category of products to display.
- sort: Specifies the sorting order for the products.
- page: Specifies the page number to display.

Accessing Query Parameters: The useRoute Composable (Again!)

To access query parameters in the component, you use the useRoute composable, just as you would for route parameters. However, instead of accessing the params property, you access the query property:

```
    import { useRoute } from 'vue-router';

export default {
  setup() {
    const route = useRoute();
    const category = route.query.category; // Access the
category parameter
    const sort = route.query.sort; // Access the sort
parameter
    const page = route.query.page || 1; // Default to page 1
if not specified

    return {
      category,
      sort,
      page
    };
  },
  template: `
    <div>
      <h2>Category: {{ category }}</h2>
      <p>Sort: {{ sort }}</p>
      <p>Page: {{ page }}</p>
    </div>
  `
};
```

Important Notes:

- **Optional Parameters:** Query parameters are optional, so you should always provide a default value in case the parameter is not specified in the URL. This can be done with the || operator like the example with page number.
- **String Values:** Query parameters are always strings, even if they represent numbers or booleans. You may need to convert them to the appropriate data type using parseInt() or Boolean().

Combining Route Parameters and Query Parameters: The Ultimate Flexibility

You can combine route parameters and query parameters in the same URL to create highly flexible and dynamic routes. For example:

```
/users/:id/posts?sort=date&order=desc
```

In this example, we're using a route parameter to specify the user ID and query parameters to specify the sorting order for the user's posts.

Programmatic Navigation with Parameters: Building Links Dynamically

To navigate to a route with parameters programmatically, you can use the router.push() method and pass an object with the name, params, and query properties:

```
    import { useRouter } from 'vue-router';

export default {
  setup() {
    const router = useRouter();

    const goToProduct = (category, productId) => {
      router.push({
        name: 'Product',
        params: { category, productId },
        query: { sort: 'price', order: 'asc' }
      });
    };
```

```
    return {
      goToProduct
    };
  },
  template: `
    <button @click="goToProduct('electronics', 123)">Go to
Product</button>
  `
};
```

This will navigate the user to the /products/electronics/123?sort=price&order=asc URL.

Personal Insight: Dynamic Routes: Unleashing the Power of SPAs

Route parameters and query parameters are what truly unlock the power of single-page applications. They allow you to create dynamic user interfaces that respond intelligently to user input and provide a personalized experience.

Conclusion: Becoming a Routing Pro

Mastering route parameters and query parameters is essential for building dynamic and user-friendly Vue.js applications. By understanding how to define dynamic routes, how to access route parameters and query parameters in your components, and how to navigate programmatically with parameters, you can create a seamless and engaging user experience. Now let's see how to protect those routes with authentication.

8.5 Route Guards – Controlling Access to Your Application's Sections: Securing Your SPA and Orchestrating Navigation

While defining routes and creating navigation links is essential for building a functional single-page application, you often need to control access to certain routes or perform specific actions before or after a user navigates to a particular route. This is where *route guards* come in.

Route guards are functions that are executed when a user tries to navigate to or from a route. They allow you to implement authentication checks, authorization rules, data validation, and other types of logic that control the navigation flow of your application. Route guards are a great tool for setting a condition for a user to pass before arriving to another route.

Think of route guards as security checkpoints along your application's roads. They ensure that only authorized users can access certain areas and that certain actions are performed before or after a user enters or leaves a specific section of the application.

Why Route Guards? Protecting Sensitive Data and Ensuring a Smooth User Experience

Route guards are essential for:

- **Authentication:** Protecting routes that require a user to be logged in.
- **Authorization:** Restricting access to certain routes based on user roles or permissions.
- **Data Validation:** Ensuring that the user has provided valid data before navigating to a route.
- **Confirmation Dialogs:** Prompting the user to confirm their action before leaving a route (e.g., if they have unsaved changes).
- **Analytics Tracking:** Logging user navigation events for analytics purposes.

Types of Route Guards: A Hierarchy of Control

Vue Router provides several types of route guards, each with a different scope and purpose:

1. **Global Before Guards:** These guards are executed before any route is activated. They are ideal for performing global authentication checks or logging user activity.
2. **Route-Specific Before Guards:** These guards are executed only before a specific route is activated. They are useful for implementing route-specific authorization rules or data validation.
3. **Component Before Guards:** These guards are defined within a component and are executed before the component is activated. They are useful for performing component-specific data validation or confirmation prompts.
4. **After Guards:** These guards are executed after a route is activated. They are useful for performing tasks such as logging user activity or updating the UI.

Understanding Guard Arguments: The to, from, and next Parameters

All route guards receive three arguments:

- **to:** The target route object that the user is trying to navigate to.
- **from:** The current route object that the user is navigating from.
- **next:** A function that you must call to resolve the navigation. The next function can be called in several ways:
    - next(): Allows the navigation to proceed to the target route.
    - next(false): Cancels the navigation and stays on the current route.
    - next('/') or next({ path: '/' }): Redirects the navigation to a different route.
    - next(error): Aborts the navigation and triggers the onError callback on the router instance.

Implementing Global Before Guards: Protecting Your Entire Application

Global before guards are registered using the router.beforeEach() method. They are executed before any route is activated, making them ideal for global authentication checks or logging user activity.

```
      import { createRouter, createWebHistory } from 'vue-
router';
import Home from '../components/Home.vue';
import About from '../components/About.vue';

const routes = [
  { path: '/', name: 'Home', component: Home },
  { path: '/about', name: 'About', component: About, meta: {
requiresAuth: true } }
];

const router = createRouter({
  history: createWebHistory(),
  routes
});

router.beforeEach((to, from, next) => {
  // Check if the route requires authentication
  if (to.meta.requiresAuth) {
    // Check if the user is logged in
    const isLoggedIn = localStorage.getItem('token');

    if (!isLoggedIn) {
```

```
      // Redirect to the login page
      next({
        path: '/login',
        query: { redirect: to.fullPath } // Store the
intended route
      });
    } else {
      // Allow access to the route
      next();
    }
  } else {
    // Allow access to the route
    next();
  }
});

export default router;
```

In this example, we're using a global before guard to protect the /about route. The to.meta.requiresAuth property is used to indicate that the route requires authentication. If the user is not logged in, they are redirected to the /login route.

Using Route Meta Fields for Configuration

Note that the requiresAuth: true property is added to the meta section of that route's config. Meta fields allow you to add extra data fields to the path for your routes. This information can then be used in the guards to give more context when allowing or disallowing access.

Route-Specific Before Guards: Fine-Grained Control

Route-specific before guards are defined directly on the route object using the beforeEnter property. They are executed only before the specific route is activated, allowing you to implement route-specific authorization rules or data validation.

```
      const routes = [
  {
    path: '/profile',
    component: Profile,
    beforeEnter: (to, from, next) => {
      // Check if the user has a valid profile
      const hasValidProfile =
localStorage.getItem('hasValidProfile');
```

```
        if (!hasValidProfile) {
          // Redirect to the profile creation page
          next('/create-profile');
        } else {
          // Allow access to the route
          next();
        }
      }
    }
];
```

In this example, we're using a route-specific before guard to protect the /profile route. The guard checks if the user has a valid profile and redirects them to the profile creation page if they don't.

Component Before Guards: Localized Control within Components

Component before guards are defined within a component using the beforeRouteEnter, beforeRouteUpdate, and beforeRouteLeave lifecycle hooks. These hooks are executed before the component is activated, updated, or deactivated, respectively.

These aren't as commonly used in Vue 3 as the first two types.

Global After Guards: Performing Actions After Navigation

After guards are registered using the router.afterEach() method. They are executed after a route is activated, allowing you to perform tasks such as logging user activity or updating the UI.

```
    router.afterEach((to, from) => {
  // Log the user's navigation
  console.log(`Navigated from ${from.path} to ${to.path}`);
});
```

Personal Insight: Route Guards: A Security Essential

Route guards have been instrumental in building secure and robust Vue.js applications. They provide a clear and concise way to control access to sensitive data and functionality, preventing unauthorized users from accessing restricted areas of the application. They act as a safeguard.

Conclusion: Guarding Your Application's Gates

Route guards are essential tools for controlling access to your Vue.js application's sections and for orchestrating navigation. By understanding the different types of route guards and how to use them effectively, you can create a secure, user-friendly, and well-behaved application. Now with the information to secure your system, let's see how to use routes to set up complex, nested component hierarchies.

8.6 Nested Routes – Organizing Complex UIs: Building Hierarchical Navigation Structures

As your Vue.js applications grow more sophisticated, you'll often need to create complex user interfaces with hierarchical layouts. Think of a dashboard application with multiple sections, each with its own set of sub-sections, or a user profile page with different tabs for profile information, settings, and activity history. Managing these structures can be a challenge.

Nested routes provide a way to organize these complex UIs by creating a hierarchy of routes, where one component is nested within another. They help keep code modular and can also assist users in getting used to a clear organizational design.

Think of nested routes as building a city with different districts, each with its own streets and buildings. The main routes represent the major districts, and the nested routes represent the streets and buildings within those districts.

The Foundation: The children Property in Route Definitions

To define nested routes, you add a children property to a route object. The children property is an array of route objects that represent the nested routes.

```
      const routes = [
  {
    path: '/users/:id',
    component: User,
    children: [
      {
        path: 'profile', // Relative path (relative to the
parent route)
        name: 'UserProfile',
        component: UserProfile
      },
      {
        path: 'settings',
```

```
        name: 'UserSettings',
        component: UserSettings
      }
    ]
  }
];
```

Key Points:

- **children Property:** The children property is an array of route objects that define the nested routes.
- **Relative Paths:** The path property of nested routes is *relative* to the parent route. In the example above, the full path for the UserProfile component would be /users/:id/profile. You can use absolute paths instead, but you need to consider your system layout, as they will be called directly and ignore the current routing path.
- **Component Hierarchy:** The component property of the parent route specifies the component that will be rendered when any of the nested routes are activated. The nested components will then be rendered *inside* the parent component.

Rendering Nested Components: The <router-view> Tag

To render the nested components, you use the <router-view> component in the parent component's template. The <router-view> component acts as a placeholder where the nested component will be rendered.

```
<template>
  <div>
    <h1>User Profile</h1>
    <nav>
      <router-link :to="{ name: 'UserProfile', params: { id: $route.params.id } }">Profile</router-link>
      <router-link :to="{ name: 'UserSettings', params: { id: $route.params.id } }">Settings</router-link>
    </nav>
    <router-view></router-view> <!-- Nested component will be rendered here -->
  </div>
</template>
```

Explanation:

- **<router-view>:** The <router-view> component acts as a placeholder where the nested component will be rendered. Vue Router will automatically render the appropriate child component inside the <router-view> based on the current URL.
- **Nested Link:** To create the nested link, the router parameters needs to get passed in to the new route. That's why it's referenced like: params: { id: $route.params.id }

Composing a Store across Multiple Component Levels:
A helpful pattern when designing the code can be to use an Inject key from a parent, so that the nested code isn't dependent on having the parent code:

```
    const injected = Symbol()

function provideMyService() {
  const data = ref(1)
  provide(injected, {
    data,
    inc: () => data.value++
  })
}

function useMyService() {
  return inject(injected)
}
```

Practical Tips: Building a Scalable Navigation Structure

- **Plan Your Route Hierarchy Carefully:** Before you start coding, take some time to plan out your application's route hierarchy. This will help you create a clear and organized navigation structure that is easy to understand and maintain.
- **Use Descriptive Route Names:** Use descriptive and meaningful names for your routes. This will make your code easier to read and understand, especially when working with programmatic navigation.
- **Use Relative Paths for Nested Routes:** Use relative paths for nested routes to keep your route definitions concise and maintainable.
- **Use the <router-view> Component for Rendering Nested Components:** Make sure to include the <router-view> component in the parent component's template to render the nested components.

Personal Insight: Nesting: Organizing Complex Interfaces

Nested routes have been invaluable for organizing complex user interfaces in my Vue.js applications. They provide a clear and structured way to manage hierarchical layouts, making it easier for users to navigate and find the information they need.

Conclusion: Building Rich and Structured Applications

Nested routes are a powerful tool for organizing complex UIs in Vue.js applications. By understanding how to define nested routes, how to render nested components, and how to create navigation links for nested routes, you can create a seamless and intuitive navigation experience for your users. With this, we have now taken a look at all the different ways to work with Routing. Congratulations!

Chapter 9: Working with APIs – Connecting Your Vue.js Application to the World

Modern web applications rarely exist in isolation. They often need to interact with external data sources, such as APIs, to retrieve information, update data, or perform other tasks. This chapter will explore how to make HTTP requests from your Vue.js application, handle API responses, display data from APIs, and manage asynchronous operations effectively.

Think of APIs as the doorways to the outside world for your Vue.js application. They allow you to connect to a vast ecosystem of data and services, enabling you to build richer, more dynamic, and more powerful applications.

9.1 Making HTTP Requests (fetch, Axios) – Choosing the Right Tool for the Job: The Foundation of API Communication

In the world of web development, communicating with external APIs is fundamental. It's how your Vue.js application retrieves data, sends updates, and interacts with other services. Making effective HTTP requests is the bedrock of API integration. There are two main ways to do that in JavaScript and Vue.js: using the built-in fetch API or using the popular third-party library, Axios.

Choosing the right tool for the job can significantly impact your development workflow and the performance of your application. This section dives into the core differences between fetch and Axios, highlighting their strengths, weaknesses, and best-use cases.

Understanding the Basics: The Purpose of HTTP Requests

HTTP (Hypertext Transfer Protocol) is the foundation of data communication on the web. It's a set of rules that govern how web browsers and servers exchange information. When your Vue.js application needs to retrieve data from an API or send data to a server, it uses HTTP requests.

Common HTTP methods include:

- **GET:** Retrieves data from a server.
- **POST:** Sends data to a server to create a new resource.
- **PUT:** Sends data to a server to update an existing resource (replaces the entire resource).
- **PATCH:** Sends data to a server to update an existing resource (modifies only specific parts of the resource).
- **DELETE:** Deletes a resource from a server.

The fetch API: Modern, Native, and Promise-Based

The fetch API is a built-in JavaScript API that provides a modern and standardized way to make HTTP requests. It's supported by all modern browsers and is based on Promises, making it easy to handle asynchronous operations.

Basic Example: Making a GET Request with fetch

```
    fetch('https://jsonplaceholder.typicode.com/todos/1')
  .then(response => {
    if (!response.ok) {
      throw new Error(`HTTP error! Status:
${response.status}`);
    }
    return response.json();
  })
  .then(data => {
    console.log('Data:', data);
  })
  .catch(error => {
    console.error('Error:', error);
  });
```

Key Characteristics of fetch:

- **Built-in:** It's a native JavaScript API, so you don't need to install any additional libraries.
- **Promise-Based:** It uses Promises for handling asynchronous operations, making it easy to chain multiple requests and handle errors.
- **Simple and Intuitive:** The API is relatively simple and easy to learn.

What's Missing? The Challenges of Using fetch

Despite its advantages, the fetch API also has some limitations:

- **Manual JSON Parsing:** You need to manually parse the response body using the response.json() method. This can be a bit tedious, especially when working with APIs that return JSON data.
- **Verbose Error Handling:** The fetch API doesn't automatically reject Promises for HTTP error status codes (400-599). You need to manually check the response.ok property and throw an error if the status code is not in the 200-299 range. This can make error handling more verbose.
- **Lacks Built-in Interceptors:** The fetch API doesn't provide a built-in mechanism for intercepting requests and responses. This can make it difficult to add global functionality, such as authentication headers or logging.
- **Older Browser Support:** You may need to add polyfills to add browser support.

Axios: The Powerful and Feature-Rich Alternative

Axios is a popular third-party library that provides a more feature-rich and flexible way to make HTTP requests. It builds on the foundation of the fetch API and adds a number of useful features that simplify common tasks.

Basic Example: Making a GET Request with Axios

```
      import axios from 'axios';

axios.get('https://jsonplaceholder.typicode.com/todos/1')
  .then(response => {
    console.log('Data:', response.data);
  })
  .catch(error => {
    console.error('Error:', error);
  });
```

Key Features of Axios:

- **Automatic JSON Transformation:** Automatically transforms the response data into JSON, eliminating the need to call response.json().
- **Global Interceptors:** Provides interceptors that allow you to modify requests and responses globally. This is useful for adding authentication headers, logging requests, or handling errors in a consistent way.

- **Progress Tracking:** Supports progress tracking for upload and download operations, allowing you to display progress bars or other visual feedback to the user.
- **Request Cancellation:** Allows you to cancel requests, which can be useful in scenarios where the user navigates away from a page before the request is completed.
- **Automatic Error Handling:** It automatically rejects the Promise if you get anything outside of the 200 status code ranges.
- **Good Browser Support:** It has broad compatibility across all sorts of browsers.

When to Choose Axios Over fetch:

- **Automatic JSON Transformation:** You need to work with JSON data frequently and want to avoid manually parsing the response body.
- **Global Interceptors:** You need to add global functionality, such as authentication headers or logging.
- **Progress Tracking:** You need to track the progress of upload or download operations.
- **Request Cancellation:** You need to be able to cancel requests.
- **Older Browser Support:** You need to support older browsers that don't fully support the fetch API.

A Head-to-Head Comparison: Key Differences at a Glance

Feature	fetch	Axios
Native Support	Yes	No (Requires installation)
JSON Transformation	Manual (response.json())	Automatic
Error Handling	Manual (Check response.ok)	Automatic (Promise rejection)
Interceptors	No	Yes
Progress Tracking	No	Yes
Request Cancellation	No	Yes
Browser Support	Modern Browsers	Wide Range of Browsers

Configuration Tips: Getting the Most Out of Axios

When using Axios, there are a few configuration options that can help you optimize your code and improve the user experience:

- **Base URL:** Define a base URL for your API in your Axios instance. This will make it easier to make requests to different endpoints on the same API.
- **Timeout:** Set a timeout for your requests to prevent them from hanging indefinitely.
- **Headers:** Set default headers, such as Content-Type and Authorization, in your Axios instance.
- **Interceptors:** Use interceptors to add global functionality, such as authentication headers or logging.

Personal Insight: Axios: A Developer's Best Friend

I've been using Axios for years, and it's become one of my go-to libraries for making HTTP requests. I appreciate its feature-rich API, its ease of use, and its ability to simplify common tasks.

Conclusion: Choosing the Right Tool for Your Needs

Both fetch and Axios are powerful tools for making HTTP requests in Vue.js applications. The choice between them depends on your specific needs and preferences. If you want a simple and lightweight solution that doesn't require any additional libraries, the fetch API is a great choice. If you need more advanced features and broader browser support, Axios is the way to go. This completes the first step in connecting to external systems, now you can handle their responses!

9.2 Handling API Responses and Errors – Responding to Success and Failure: The Art of Graceful API Communication

Making HTTP requests is only half the battle. What happens when the API responds? Properly handling both successful responses and potential errors is paramount for building robust, reliable, and user-friendly Vue.js applications. A smooth and intuitive API experience hinges on handling what comes back.

This section focuses on the best practices for handling API responses and errors, ensuring that your application can gracefully handle both expected and unexpected scenarios.

Understanding the Landscape: API Responses – Decoding the Server's Message

When you make an API request, the server responds with a set of data. This response typically includes:

- **Status Code:** A numerical code that indicates the success or failure of the request. Status codes in the 200-299 range indicate success, while status codes in the 400-599 range indicate an error.
- **Headers:** Metadata about the response, such as the content type, content length, and caching instructions.
- **Body:** The actual data returned by the server. This is often in JSON format, but it can also be in other formats, such as XML or plain text.

Successful Responses: Parsing and Using the Data

When an API call is successful (status code in the 200-299 range), you need to parse the response body and extract the data that you need. This typically involves using the response.json() method to convert the JSON data into a JavaScript object or array. (Axios does this automatically, but you need to do so for fetch.)

```
    fetch('https://jsonplaceholder.typicode.com/todos/1')
  .then(response => {
    if (!response.ok) {
      throw new Error(`HTTP error! Status:
${response.status}`);
    }
    return response.json();
  })
  .then(data => {
    console.log('Data:', data);
    // Display the data in your UI
  })
  .catch(error => {
    console.error('Error:', error);
    // Handle the error
  });
```

Once you've parsed the data, you can update your component's state and display the data in your template.

The Inevitable: Handling Errors with Resilience

Even with the best planning and code, errors can and will occur when working with APIs. It's crucial to anticipate these errors and handle them gracefully to prevent your application from crashing and to provide a good user experience.

Common Error Scenarios:

- **Network Connectivity Issues:** The user's internet connection may be down or unstable.
- **Server Errors:** The API server may be down or experiencing problems.
- **Client-Side Errors:** The request may be malformed, the user may not have the necessary permissions, or the API may return an unexpected response.

Error Handling Strategies: A Multi-Layered Approach

A robust error handling strategy typically involves several layers:

1. **try...catch Blocks:** Wrap your API calls in try...catch blocks to catch any exceptions that may be thrown during the request or response processing.
2. **Checking Response Status Codes:** Inspect the HTTP status code of the response to determine if the request was successful. Remember that fetch requires you to manually check this.
3. **Providing Informative Error Messages:** If an error occurs, display an informative error message to the user that helps them understand what went wrong and what they can do to fix it.
4. **Logging Errors to the Server:** Log errors to the server so that you can track them and identify any recurring issues.
5. **Implementing Retry Mechanisms:** For transient errors, such as network connectivity issues, consider implementing a retry mechanism that automatically retries the request after a certain period of time.

A Practical Example: Fetching Data with Error Handling

Let's revisit our example of fetching data from an API and add robust error handling:

```
      import { ref, onMounted } from 'vue';
import axios from 'axios';

export default {
  setup() {
    const todo = ref(null);
    const loading = ref(true);
    const errorMessage = ref('');

    const fetchData = async () => {
      try {
        const response = await
axios.get('https://jsonplaceholder.typicode.com/todos/1');
        todo.value = response.data;
        errorMessage.value = ''; // Clear any previous error
message
      } catch (error) {
        console.error('Error fetching data:', error);
        errorMessage.value = 'Failed to fetch data. Please
check your connection and try again.';
      } finally {
        loading.value = false;
      }
    };

    onMounted(fetchData);

    return {
      todo,
      loading,
      errorMessage
    };
  },
  template: `
    <div>
      <p v-if="loading">Loading...</p>
      <p v-else-if="errorMessage">Error: {{ errorMessage
}}</p>
      <div v-else>
        <h2>{{ todo.title }}</h2>
        <p>Completed: {{ todo.completed }}</p>
      </div>
    </div>
  `
};
```

Explanation:

1. **try...catch Block:** We wrap the API call in a try...catch block to catch any exceptions that may be thrown.
2. **Informative Error Message:** If an error occurs, we set the errorMessage ref to an informative error message that is displayed to the user.
3. **Clearing Previous Errors:** If the fetch succeeds, the error message is cleared.
4. **finally Block:** The finally block ensures that the loading ref is always set to false, regardless of whether the request was successful or not.

HTTP Status Codes: Interpreting the Server's Response

HTTP status codes provide valuable information about the outcome of an API request. It's helpful to think about what these different codes might mean.

Common Status Code Ranges:

- **200-299 (Success):** The request was successful.
- **300-399 (Redirection):** The resource has been moved or redirected.
- **400-499 (Client Error):** The request was malformed or the client is not authorized to access the resource.
- **500-599 (Server Error):** The server encountered an error while processing the request.

Personal Insight: Never Trust the Network

One of the most important lessons I've learned as a web developer is to "never trust the network." Network connections are unreliable, servers can go down, and APIs can return unexpected responses. It's essential to build your applications with these realities in mind and to implement robust error handling to ensure a smooth user experience.

Conclusion: Ensuring a Smooth and Reliable API Experience

Handling API responses and errors effectively is crucial for building robust and user-friendly Vue.js applications. By following the principles and techniques outlined in this section, you can create applications that gracefully handle both successful responses and potential errors, providing a seamless and reliable experience for your users. Next, let's see how we can use and display that data!

9.3 Displaying Data from APIs – Bringing Data to Life: From Raw Response to Engaging UI

Fetching data from an API is only the first step. The real magic happens when you take that raw data and transform it into a compelling and user-friendly interface. This section explores how to effectively display API data in your Vue.js application, making it accessible, engaging, and easy to understand for your users. You can think of a designer having a specific purpose and look for certain types of data to get the most engaging results.

Think of displaying API data as painting a picture with data. You need to choose the right colors, arrange the elements in a visually appealing way, and add context to make the data meaningful and engaging for your audience.

Key Techniques: From Data to DOM

Here's a rundown of the most common and effective techniques for displaying API data in Vue.js:

1. **Data Binding: Seamlessly Connecting Data to the Template:**

   The foundation of displaying data in Vue.js is data binding. This involves using Vue's template syntax to connect data properties in your component to elements in the HTML template.

   - **Interpolation:** Use double curly braces {{ }} to display simple data values.

```
<h2>{{ todo.title }}</h2>
<p>Completed: {{ todo.completed }}</p>
```

   - **Attribute Binding:** Use the v-bind directive (or its shorthand :) to dynamically set HTML attributes based on data properties.

```
<img :src="imageUrl" :alt="imageAltText">
```

2. **Conditional Rendering: Displaying Data Selectively**

   Often, you'll want to display different content based on the value of a data property. This is where conditional rendering comes in. Use the v-if, v-else-if, and v-else directives to conditionally render elements based on a boolean expression.

```
<p v-if="isLoading">Loading...</p>
<div v-else-if="error">Error: {{ error }}</div>
<div v-else>
  <!-- Display the data -->
</div>
```

3. **List Rendering: Iterating Over Data Collections**

   When working with APIs, you'll often receive data in the form of arrays. The v-for directive allows you to iterate over these arrays and render a list of elements.

```
<ul>
  <li v-for="item in items" :key="item.id">{{ item.name
}}</li>
</ul>
```

4. **Data Formatting: Transforming Raw Data into Human-Readable Information**

   Sometimes, the data you receive from an API may not be in the desired format for display. You may need to format dates, numbers, currencies, or other data types to make them more readable and user-friendly.

   - **JavaScript's Built-in Methods:** Use JavaScript's built-in methods for formatting data.

```
const date = new Date('2023-10-27T12:00:00Z');
const formattedDate = date.toLocaleDateString(); //
"10/27/2023"
```

- **Third-Party Libraries:** Use third-party libraries like Moment.js or date-fns for more advanced date formatting.

```
import moment from 'moment';

const date = moment('2023-10-27T12:00:00Z');
const formattedDate = date.format('MMMM D, YYYY'); //
"October 27, 2023"
```

A Practical Example: Displaying a To-Do List from an API

Let's put these techniques into practice with a complete example of displaying a to-do list from an API:

```
<template>
  <div>
    <h1>To-Do List</h1>
    <p v-if="loading">Loading...</p>
    <p v-else-if="error">Error: {{ error }}</p>
    <ul v-else>
      <li v-for="todo in todos" :key="todo.id">
        {{ todo.title }} -
        <span v-if="todo.completed">Completed</span>
        <span v-else>Incomplete</span>
      </li>
    </ul>
  </div>
</template>

<script>
import { ref, onMounted } from 'vue';
import axios from 'axios';

export default {
  setup() {
    const todos = ref([]);
    const loading = ref(true);
    const error = ref('');

    const fetchTodos = async () => {
      try {
        const response = await
axios.get('https://jsonplaceholder.typicode.com/todos');
        todos.value = response.data.slice(0, 10); // Limit to
10 items for brevity
      } catch (error) {
        console.error('Error fetching todos:', error);
```

```
        error.value = 'Failed to fetch to-dos. Please try
again later.';
      } finally {
        loading.value = false;
      }
    };

    onMounted(fetchTodos);

    return {
      todos,
      loading,
      error
    };
  }
};
</script>
```

Explanation:

1. **Fetching the Data:** The fetchTodos function fetches an array of to-do items from the JSONPlaceholder API.
2. **Loading and Error Handling:** We use loading and error refs to handle the loading state and any potential errors.
3. **Data Binding:** We use {{ todo.title }} to display the title of each to-do item.
4. **Conditional Rendering:** We use v-if and v-else to display a loading indicator, an error message, or the list of to-do items, depending on the current state.
5. **List Rendering:** We use v-for to iterate over the todos array and render a list of to-do items.

The Importance of User Experience

When displaying data from APIs, it's crucial to consider the user experience. Think about how you can present the data in a way that is clear, concise, and easy to understand. Use appropriate formatting, visual cues, and interactive elements to make the data more engaging and user-friendly.

Personal Insight: Data Transformation: A Key Skill

I've learned that mastering the art of data transformation is essential for building successful Vue.js applications. The data you receive from APIs is rarely in the perfect format for display. You need to be able to transform the data into a format that is both technically correct and visually appealing.

Conclusion: From API to Engaging UI

Displaying data from APIs is a core skill for any Vue.js developer. By understanding how to use data binding, conditional rendering, list rendering, and data formatting, you can create user interfaces that are both informative and engaging. Finally, let's discuss how we can use async functions.

9.4 Asynchronous Operations with async/await – Simplifying Asynchronous Code: Taming the Asynchronous Beast

Asynchronous operations are an unavoidable part of modern web development, particularly when working with APIs. Making API calls, handling user input, and performing complex calculations can all take time, and you don't want to block the main thread and make your UI unresponsive.

The async/await syntax in JavaScript provides a powerful and elegant way to handle asynchronous operations in a more synchronous-looking style.

Think of async/await as a set of traffic lights that help you manage the flow of asynchronous code. It allows you to pause the execution of a function until a Promise resolves, making your code easier to read, understand, and maintain.

Understanding the Problem: The Callback Hell and Promise Chains

Before async/await, asynchronous operations were typically handled using callbacks or Promise chains. While these approaches work, they can quickly become complex and difficult to read, especially when dealing with multiple asynchronous operations.

Callback hell is a situation where you have deeply nested callbacks, making your code look like a pyramid or an arrow. Promise chains can also become difficult to read and maintain as they grow in length and complexity.

The Solution: async/await – A More Synchronous Approach

The async/await syntax simplifies asynchronous code by allowing you to write it in a more synchronous-looking style. Instead of using callbacks or Promise chains, you can simply use the await keyword to wait for a Promise to resolve.

Key Concepts: async Functions and await Expressions

- **async Functions:** To use the await keyword, you must first declare a function as async. The async keyword tells JavaScript that the function will contain asynchronous operations and that it should automatically wrap the function's return value in a Promise.

```
async function fetchData() {
  // Asynchronous code here
}
```

- **await Expressions:** The await keyword is used to pause the execution of an async function until a Promise resolves. The await keyword can only be used inside async functions.

```
async function fetchData() {
  const response = await
fetch('https://jsonplaceholder.typicode.com/todos/1'); //
Wait for the Promise to resolve
  const data = await response.json(); // Wait for the Promise
to resolve
  console.log(data);
}
```

How It Works: Behind the Scenes

When you use the await keyword, JavaScript effectively pauses the execution of the async function until the Promise resolves. During this time, the browser is free to perform other tasks, such as updating the UI or responding to user input. Once the Promise resolves, JavaScript resumes the execution of the async function at the point where it was paused.

Practical Example: Fetching Data with async/await and Error Handling

Let's revisit our example of fetching data from an API and use async/await to simplify the code:

```
      import { ref, onMounted } from 'vue';
import axios from 'axios';

export default {
  setup() {
    const todo = ref(null);
    const loading = ref(true);
    const errorMessage = ref('');

    const fetchData = async () => {
      try {
        const response = await
axios.get('https://jsonplaceholder.typicode.com/todos/1'); //
Await the response
        todo.value = response.data;
        errorMessage.value = ''; // Clear any previous error
message
      } catch (error) {
        console.error('Error fetching data:', error);
        errorMessage.value = 'Failed to fetch data. Please
check your connection and try again.';
      } finally {
        loading.value = false;
      }
    };

    onMounted(fetchData);

    return {
      todo,
      loading,
      errorMessage
    };
  },
  template: `
    <div>
      <p v-if="loading">Loading...</p>
      <p v-else-if="errorMessage">Error: {{ errorMessage
}}</p>
      <div v-else>
        <h2>{{ todo.title }}</h2>
        <p>Completed: {{ todo.completed }}</p>
      </div>
    </div>
  `
};
```

Explanation:

- **async fetchData():** Declares the fetchData function as asynchronous.
- **await axios.get(...):** Pauses the execution of the function until the axios.get() Promise resolves.
- **await response.data:** Pauses the execution of the function until data is returned.
- **try...catch Block:** Handles any errors that may occur during the asynchronous operation.

Benefits of Using async/await:

- **Improved Readability:** Makes asynchronous code look and feel synchronous, making it easier to read and understand.
- **Simplified Error Handling:** Simplifies error handling by allowing you to use try...catch blocks to catch errors that may occur during asynchronous operations.
- **Easier Debugging:** Makes debugging asynchronous code easier by allowing you to step through the code line by line using a debugger.

Combining async/await with Other Techniques:

You can combine async/await with other techniques, such as Promise.all() and Promise.race(), to perform more complex asynchronous operations.

Personal Insight: Async/Await: A Step Forward for Developers

The async/await syntax has been a significant improvement in the way I write asynchronous code. It has made my code more readable, easier to understand, and less prone to errors. It's one of those features that once you start using, you can't imagine going back to the old way of doing things.

Conclusion: Mastering Asynchronous Operations with Style

The world of the async function does not have to be scary! By following these concepts, your codebase can come alive!

Chapter 10: Advanced Component Patterns – Unlocking the Full Power of Vue.js

In the previous chapters, we've covered the fundamentals of Vue.js, including components, reactivity, and state management. Now, it's time to explore more advanced component patterns that will empower you to build more sophisticated and flexible applications. This chapter is about going beyond the basics and taking your Vue.js skills to the next level.

These techniques can bring more creativity and power to your project. This chapter brings into focus:

- Teleport: Rendering Elements outside of the component scope
- Suspense: Helping components load without freezing out the User Interface
- Directives: A more in depth dive into directives, and how to customize them.
- Transitions and Animations: A look at making your UI shine with animation!

10.1 Teleport: Rendering Outside the DOM – Breaking Free from the Component Hierarchy: Taking Control of DOM Structure

In the world of Vue.js development, components are the building blocks of your application's user interface. But, you will find that with just components alone, the DOM becomes very limited and a challenge to work with. Components can often lead to deeply nested structures, and you can't always control where a component's output is rendered within the DOM tree. Sometimes, you need the ability to break free from the component hierarchy and render content in a different part of the DOM, outside of the current component's parent element. This is where the <teleport> component comes to the rescue.

<teleport> allows us to break away from that structure in a good way. This component allows you to "teleport" a portion of your template to a completely different part of the DOM.

Think of <teleport> as a portal that allows you to send a piece of your component's output to a specific location in the DOM, regardless of where the component itself is located. This is like having a remote control that allows you to move elements around in the DOM tree with ease.

Why Teleport? Solving Common UI Challenges

Teleport solves a number of common UI challenges:

- **Modal Dialogs:** Modals often need to be rendered at the top level of the DOM (e.g., as direct children of the <body> element) to avoid styling or positioning issues caused by parent elements.
- **Tooltips and Popovers:** Similar to modals, tooltips and popovers often need to be positioned relative to the viewport, regardless of their parent component's position.
- **Full-Screen Overlays:** Elements, such as loading indicators or error messages, may need to cover the entire screen, regardless of the component hierarchy.
- **Accessibility:** Teleporting content to a more appropriate location in the DOM can improve accessibility for users with disabilities.

The Basics: Using the <teleport> Component

To use Teleport, you wrap the content that you want to teleport inside a <teleport> component. The <teleport> component has a single required prop:

- **to:** Specifies the target element where you want to render the content. The value of the to prop should be a valid CSS selector (e.g., "body", "#modal-container", ".my-element").

Here's a basic example:

```
    <template>
<div>
  <button @click="showModal = true">Open Modal</button>

  <teleport to="body">
    <div v-if="showModal" class="modal">
      <h2>Modal Title</h2>
      <p>Modal Content</p>
      <button @click="showModal = false">Close</button>
    </div>
  </teleport>
</div>
```

```
</template>

<script>
import { ref } from 'vue';

export default {
  setup() {
    const showModal = ref(false);

    return {
      showModal
    };
  }
};
</script>

<style scoped>
.modal {
  position: fixed;
  top: 50%;
  left: 50%;
  transform: translate(-50%, -50%);
  background-color: white;
  padding: 20px;
  border: 1px solid #ccc;
  box-shadow: 0 0 10px rgba(0, 0, 0, 0.2);
  z-index: 1000;
}
</style>
```

Understanding the Code:

1. **<teleport to="body">:** This tells Vue to render the content inside the <teleport> component at the end of the <body> element.
2. **v-if="showModal":** This conditionally renders the modal content only when the showModal ref is true.
3. **Scoped Styles:** The scoped attribute on the <style> tag ensures that the styles for the modal component only apply to that component and don't affect other parts of the application.

Why Teleport to body? Addressing Common Styling Issues

Teleporting to the body is a common practice for modals and other floating elements because it helps to avoid styling conflicts with parent elements. Parent elements may have styles that affect the positioning, z-index, overflow, or other visual properties of the modal, which can lead to unexpected results.

By teleporting to the body, you ensure that the modal is rendered at the top level of the DOM, outside of any potentially conflicting styles.

Teleporting to Other Elements: Flexibility Beyond body

While teleporting to the body is a common use case, you can teleport content to any element in the DOM that matches the specified CSS selector. This allows you to create more complex layouts and to position elements more precisely.

Multiple Teleports: Handling Multiple Destinations

You can use multiple <teleport> components to render content to different locations in the DOM. This can be useful for creating complex layouts with multiple floating elements or for rendering content in different parts of the page based on the user's screen size.

Personal Insight: Teleport: A Styling Superpower

I can't stress how helpful Teleport has been. For modal dialogs, I needed to make sure the content was on top of everything (zIndex), but other elements had zIndexes set to them. Now instead of having to keep track, I can just set the Teleport to be in the base application, outside of all other components. Teleport also helps to keep my styling local, and avoid having to worry about the cascading effects.

Advanced Use Cases: Teleporting Components, Not Just Templates

You can even teleport entire components, not just snippets of templates. This can be particularly useful when you want to create reusable components that can be rendered in different parts of the application without modifying their internal logic.

TypeScript Considerations: Type Safety with Teleport

When working with TypeScript, you can add type annotations to your Teleport components to ensure type safety:

Conclusion: Mastering DOM Placement with Teleport

Teleport is a powerful and essential tool for building complex and user-friendly Vue.js applications. By understanding how to use the <teleport> component, how to specify the target element, and how to handle styling and event handling, you can create user interfaces that are both visually appealing and easy to maintain. Let's move on to something to let users know when the app is still loading.

10.2 Suspense: Handling Asynchronous Components – Providing a Graceful Loading Experience: From Blank Screens to Engaging Progress

In the age of data-driven web applications, asynchronous components are the norm. We frequently load data from APIs, process images, or perform other time-consuming tasks before rendering a component's content. However, this can lead to a jarring user experience if the component takes too long to load. Users are left with a blank screen, wondering if something went wrong or if the application is even working.

The <Suspense> component in Vue 3 provides a way to address this issue by allowing you to display a fallback content while an asynchronous component is loading. This creates a more seamless and engaging user experience, preventing the UI from feeling slow or unresponsive.

Think of <Suspense> as a content gatekeeper. When your lazy data needs to load before showing the component, it makes sure to keep the door closed until everything is ready!

The Core Concept: Suspense - Adding the loading screen

The key to using <Suspense> lies in wrapping async components in the Suspense tag. This tag gives you two slots:

1. #default: Displays once the component's asynchronous data and code have loaded.
2. #fallback: Displays if data has not yet loaded.
   These are set like so:

```
<template>
<div>
  <Suspense>
    <template #default>
```

```
        <MyAsyncComponent />
      </template>
      <template #fallback>
        <div>Loading...</div>
      </template>
    </Suspense>
  </div>
</template>
```

Using defineAsyncComponent:

For a component to work with Suspense, it needs to be defined as an asynchronous component using defineAsyncComponent. This informs Vue that the component's code and data may not be immediately available. Vue will use this information to manage the loading state and display the appropriate content.
This looks like:

```
      import { defineAsyncComponent } from 'vue';

const MyAsyncComponent = defineAsyncComponent(() =>
import('./MyComponent.vue'));

export default {
  components: {
    MyAsyncComponent
  }
};
```

Let's combine that into one complete example:

```
      <template>
  <div>
    <Suspense>
      <template #default>
        <MyAsyncComponent />
      </template>
      <template #fallback>
        <div>Loading...</div>
      </template>
    </Suspense>
  </div>
</template>

<script>
import { defineAsyncComponent } from 'vue';
```

```
const MyAsyncComponent = defineAsyncComponent(() =>
import('./MyComponent.vue'));

export default {
  components: {
    MyAsyncComponent
  }
};
</script>
```

Practical Tips: Providing a User-Friendly Loading Experience

- **Use Meaningful Fallback Content:** Don't just display a generic "Loading..." message. Provide more informative fallback content that gives the user an idea of what to expect.
- **Use Skeleton Screens:** Skeleton screens are a great way to provide a visual representation of the loading component's layout. They show the user where the data will be displayed once it's loaded, giving them a sense of progress.
- **Handle Errors Gracefully:** Use the error hook to handle any errors that may occur while loading the asynchronous component. Display an informative error message to the user and provide options to retry the loading process or contact support.

Combining Suspense with Transitions: A Seamless Visual Experience

You can combine <Suspense> with the <transition> component to create a seamless visual transition between the fallback content and the loaded component. This can help to reduce the jarring effect of the content suddenly appearing on the screen.

Personal Insight: Suspense - From Frowns to Smiles

I have used Suspense in a variety of projects to smooth the User Experience. By preventing the user from seeing a big blank screen, Vue's design becomes more modern and engaging!

Conclusion: Taking the User Experience to Another Dimension

Suspense makes asynchronous loading screens a breeze. By taking it into consideration, you can make applications that are dynamic and responsive. Let's keep our journey moving towards custom directives.

10.3 Custom Directives: Extending Vue's Functionality – Tailoring the Framework to Your Needs: Beyond the Built-In - Crafting Your Own DOM Superpowers

Vue.js comes packed with handy built-in directives like v-if, v-for, v-model, and v-bind. However, sometimes you need to perform more complex DOM manipulations or add custom behavior that isn't covered by these built-in directives. This is where custom directives shine.

Think of custom directives as a way to extend Vue's vocabulary, adding new HTML attributes that you can use to declaratively manipulate the DOM. They allow you to encapsulate DOM-related logic and reuse it throughout your application, making your code more modular, maintainable, and expressive. They are also an excellent tool to help bridge the code, and styling concerns.

What Are Custom Directives? Giving HTML New Tricks

Custom directives let you add custom behavior to HTML elements. In a nutshell, it connects directly to some code you created!

Key uses for directives are:

- Reusable Code
- DOM Access
- Abstraction: Simplifying complex tasks.
- Readability

Creating a Custom Directive: The Essential Ingredients

To define a custom directive, you use the directive API on the Vue app instance:

```
      const app = Vue.createApp(App)

app.directive('my-directive', {
  // directive hooks
})
```

Understanding Directive Hooks: Tapping into the DOM Lifecycle

Custom directives have a set of lifecycle hooks that are called at different stages of the element's lifecycle. These hooks allow you to perform specific actions at the right time, such as setting up event listeners, modifying the element's attributes, or performing other DOM manipulations.

Here's a breakdown of the available lifecycle hooks:

- **created(el, binding, vnode, prevVnode):** Called before the bound element's attributes or event listeners are applied.
    - el: The element the directive is bound to.
    - binding: An object that contains information about the directive, such as its name, value, modifiers, and arguments.
    - vnode: The virtual node representing the bound element.
    - prevVnode: The previous virtual node (only available in beforeUpdate and updated).
- **beforeMount(el, binding, vnode, prevVnode):** Called when the directive is bound to the element and before the element is inserted into the DOM.
- **mounted(el, binding, vnode, prevVnode):** Called when the directive is bound to the element and the element has been inserted into the DOM. This is a great place to perform tasks that require access to the DOM, such as setting up event listeners or initializing third-party libraries.
- **beforeUpdate(el, binding, vnode, prevVnode):** Called before the component containing the element has updated, but potentially before any DOM updates have been applied. This can be useful for accessing the previous DOM state.
- **updated(el, binding, vnode, prevVnode):** Called after the component containing the element and the DOM have updated. This can be used to perform tasks that require access to the updated DOM state.
- **beforeUnmount(el, binding, vnode, prevVnode):** Called before the component containing the element has been unmounted. This is the perfect place for cleanup.
- **unmounted(el, binding, vnode, prevVnode):** Called when the directive is unbound from the element and the parent component is unmounted. This is the last chance to perform any cleanup tasks.

Simple Custom Directive: v-focus - Give The People What They Want

Let's create a simple example of a v-focus directive that automatically focuses an input element when it is inserted into the DOM:

```
const app = Vue.createApp(App)

app.directive('focus', {
  mounted(el) {
    el.focus()
  }
})
```

Using the v-focus Directive

To use the custom directive, simply add it as an attribute to the DOM element:

```
<template>
  <div>
    <input type="text" v-focus />
  </div>
</template>
```

When the component is mounted, the v-focus directive will automatically focus the input element, making it ready for user input.

Custom Directives and Arguments: Providing Data

Let's see about connecting external data, not just functions. With the code, here's how you pass custom data and arguments to your directives!

```
<p v-highlight="'yellow'">Highlight this text!</p>
```

Now our goal is to customize a directive with its code.

Accessing the data in the directives code

To access the argument value in the directive's lifecycle hooks, you use the binding.value property:

```
app.directive('highlight', {
  mounted(el, binding) {
    el.style.backgroundColor = binding.value
  }
})
```

Personal insight: Custom Directives are where Design and Code Meet!
I recall working on a project where the designer gave a long spec that would take 4 steps to get to the final result. I tried using basic HTML, but with the help of directives, I was able to cut down on HTML, make the system simpler, and get the same results that the designer wanted!

Bringing it all together, a helpful example

Here's a helpful directive that connects data to the styling of the image!
(It also has the helpful tool of throwing an error when the image doesn't load.
)

```
    app.directive('img-fallback', {
  mounted(el, binding) {
    const loadImage = () => {
      el.src = binding.value
    }
    const handleError = () => {
      el.src = binding.arg // set fallback image
    }

    el.addEventListener('load', loadImage)
    el.addEventListener('error', handleError)
  },
  unmounted(el, binding) {
    el.removeEventListener('load', this.loadImage)
    el.removeEventListener('error', this.handleError)
  }
})
```

And the calling tag:

```
    <img
  v-img-fallback:https://i.imgur.com/VxJ1P3A.jpeg
  src="https://this-image-does-not-exist.com"
  alt="The landscape"
/>
```

Conclusion: The Sky's the Limit

Custom directives provide a powerful way to extend Vue's functionality. By understanding how to define custom directives, how to use lifecycle hooks, and how to pass arguments to directives, you can create a set of reusable

DOM manipulations that are tailored to your specific application needs. Now, to wrap it all up and tie it nicely, let's talk about transitions.

10.4 Transitions and Animations – Bringing Your UI to Life: Adding Delight and Polish to Your Vue.js Applications

A well-designed user interface is not just about functionality; it's also about creating a delightful and engaging experience for your users. Transitions and animations are a powerful tool for achieving this, adding a sense of motion, providing feedback on user actions, and making your application feel more polished and professional.

This section explores how to add transitions and animations to your Vue.js applications using the built-in <transition> component and related features. These techniques can breathe life into your UI, making it more appealing and intuitive for your users.

Understanding the Basics: Transitions vs. Animations

Before diving into the code, it's helpful to understand the difference between transitions and animations:

- **Transitions:** Typically involve animating changes in CSS properties over a short period of time (e.g., fading in an element, sliding an element into view). They are often triggered by changes in the component's state or by user interactions.
- **Animations:** More complex and customizable than transitions. They involve animating multiple CSS properties over a longer period of time and can be controlled with keyframes. Animations are often used to create more elaborate and eye-catching effects.

The <transition> Component: Animating Visibility Changes

The <transition> component is Vue's primary mechanism for adding transitions to your components. It automatically applies CSS classes to the element being transitioned, allowing you to define the transition's starting and ending states using CSS.

To use the <transition> component, you simply wrap the element that you want to animate inside the <transition> component:

```
<template>
  <div>
    <button @click="show = !show">Toggle</button>
    <transition name="fade">
      <p v-if="show">Hello, world!</p>
    </transition>
  </div>
</template>

<script>
import { ref } from 'vue';

export default {
  setup() {
    const show = ref(false);

    return {
      show
    };
  }
};
</script>

<style scoped>
.fade-enter-active,
.fade-leave-active {
  transition: opacity 0.5s ease;
}

.fade-enter-from,
.fade-leave-to {
  opacity: 0;
}
</style>
```

How It Works: The Transition Class Names

The <transition> component automatically applies CSS classes to the element during the transition. These classes are used to define the transition's starting and ending states.

By default, the <transition> component uses the following class names:

- **v-enter-from:** Applied before the element is inserted into the DOM and removed after one frame. Use this to define the starting state of the transition.

- **v-enter-active:** Applied when the element is being inserted into the DOM. Use this to define the transition duration, timing function, and other transition properties.
- **v-enter-to:** Applied after the element has been inserted into the DOM. Use this to define the ending state of the transition.
- **v-leave-from:** Applied when the element is being removed from the DOM. Use this to define the starting state of the transition.
- **v-leave-active:** Applied when the element is being removed from the DOM. Use this to define the transition duration, timing function, and other transition properties.
- **v-leave-to:** Applied after the element has been removed from the DOM. Use this to define the ending state of the transition.

You can customize these class names by using the name prop on the <transition> component. In the example above, we're using the name="fade" prop, which tells Vue to use the following class names:

- fade-enter-from
- fade-enter-active
- fade-enter-to
- fade-leave-from
- fade-leave-active
- fade-leave-to

Animating Transitions
Note that it works with just the basic css you already know!

Understanding Mode Types: Making Transitions More Controlled

Vue offers the option to define a mode for the transition. The default mode for the transition works when there is nothing to transition. But for more detailed actions, then more modes need to be implemented.

They key modes are:

- **in-out**: Transition for enter is performed first, then exit.
- **out-in**: Transition for leave is performed first, then enter.

The enter is typically performed first, but when you have more complicated transitions, you may want the exit to appear first.
Here's a quick example:

```
    <template>
  <button @click="show = !show">
    Toggle render
  </button>

  <Transition name="slide" mode="out-in">
    <p v-if="show">
      Slide Transition
    </p>
  </Transition>
</template>

<style>
.slide-enter-active {
  transition: all 0.3s ease-out;
}

.slide-leave-active {
  transition: all 0.8s cubic-bezier(1, 0.5, 0.8, 1);
}

.slide-enter-from {
  transform: translateX(10px);
  opacity: 0;
}

.slide-leave-to {
  transform: translateX(-10px);
  opacity: 0;
}
</style>
```

Animations: Creating More Complex Effects with Keyframes

For more complex animations, you can use CSS animations with keyframes. Keyframes allow you to define multiple states for an animation and to specify how the animation should transition between those states.

Personal Insight: Animations - Make The Project Stand Out

To me it doesn't matter how simple a website is, as long as it has the right animations to give the user a satisfying experience. That's a big part of why it's a cornerstone of web development.

Conclusion: Enhancing Your User Interface with Motion

Transitions and animations are powerful tools for enhancing the user experience in your Vue.js applications. By understanding how to use the <transition> component, CSS transitions, and CSS animations, you can create user interfaces that are both visually appealing and engaging. This concludes the advance section, moving on to testing the application.

Chapter 11: Testing Your Vue.js Applications – Building Confidence in Your Code

Testing is a crucial part of the software development process, and Vue.js applications are no exception. Writing tests helps you ensure that your code is working correctly, that it continues to work correctly as you make changes, and that your application is reliable and maintainable. This chapter covers the fundamentals of testing Vue.js applications, and how to make code robust!

This chapter aims to help you create:

- Unit Tests: Verifying the output of individual code functions.
- Component Tests: Ensures that each independent component works well.
- End-to-End Testing: A look at how to test a fully created system.

11.1 Introduction to Testing – Why Test?: Building a Foundation of Confidence in Your Code

In the world of software development, the word "testing" often conjures images of tedious tasks, bug hunts, and late nights spent fixing unexpected issues. However, at its core, testing is not just about finding bugs; it's about building *confidence* in your code. It's about ensuring that your application works as expected, that it continues to work as you make changes, and that it provides a reliable and consistent user experience.

This section explores the fundamental reasons why testing is an essential part of the software development process, providing a clear understanding of the benefits and value that testing brings to your Vue.js projects.

The Importance of Testing: Beyond Bug Hunting

While finding and fixing bugs is a crucial aspect of testing, the benefits extend far beyond simply identifying errors. A robust testing strategy can significantly improve the overall quality, maintainability, and scalability of your applications.

Here are the key reasons why testing is so important:

- **Early Bug Detection:** Tests help you identify bugs early in the development process, before they make their way into production. The earlier you find a bug, the easier and cheaper it is to fix. Bugs caught in production can be extremely difficult and expensive to resolve.
- **Regression Prevention:** Tests help you ensure that new changes don't break existing functionality. As you add new features or refactor your code, tests act as a safety net, alerting you to any unintended consequences.
- **Improved Code Quality:** Writing tests forces you to think about the design of your code and to write more modular, testable, and maintainable code. Testable code is typically well-organized, loosely coupled, and easy to understand.
- **Increased Confidence:** Tests give you confidence that your code is working correctly, allowing you to make changes and deploy new features with greater peace of mind. When code isn't tested, you can't be sure that you didn't break something.
- **Living Documentation:** Well-written tests can serve as a form of documentation, showing how your code is intended to be used and how it should behave in different scenarios. A test shows what you expect as a result.

Testing as a Design Tool: Guiding Development Decisions

The act of writing tests can also serve as a powerful design tool. By thinking about how you're going to test your code *before* you write it, you're forced to consider the inputs, outputs, and edge cases of your functions and components. This can lead to better design decisions and more robust code.

The Simple Goal: Test Before You Ship

The goal of writing tests is simple: to help your team to be more confident in every release. That confidence can enable them to build more features.

A Concrete Analogy: Building a Bridge

Imagine building a bridge designed to handle heavy traffic.

- **Without Tests:** You might construct the bridge based solely on theoretical calculations, hoping everything will hold up. However, you'd have no concrete evidence to back up your assumptions.

- **With Tests:** You'd subject the bridge to a series of rigorous tests, such as stress tests, load tests, and stability tests, to verify that it can withstand the intended loads and environmental conditions. This would give you much greater confidence in the bridge's safety and reliability.

Code is much the same. You can follow best practices, but until tests are present to prove their veracity, the code is untested.

The Testing Pyramid: A Strategic Approach

There are many different types of tests, each with its own purpose and scope. A common way to visualize the different types of tests is the testing pyramid.

The testing pyramid suggests that you should have a large number of low-level tests (unit tests), a moderate number of mid-level tests (integration tests or component tests), and a small number of high-level tests (end-to-end tests).

1. **Unit Tests:** These tests target small, isolated units of code, such as functions or methods. They are fast to run and easy to write, making them ideal for catching basic errors and ensuring that your code is behaving as expected.
2. **Component Tests:** These tests verify the behavior of individual components, including their templates, props, events, and state. They are more comprehensive than unit tests, but they are also slower to run.
3. **End-to-End (E2E) Tests:** These tests simulate real user interactions with your application, verifying that the entire system is working correctly from the user's perspective. They are the most comprehensive type of test, but they are also the slowest to run and the most difficult to write.

Tools: The Tools for Testing that do the Job

We will mostly be looking at the different tools at your disposal.

- **Jest:** A JavaScript testing framework that provides a complete set of tools for writing unit tests, integration tests, and end-to-end tests. Jest is known for its ease of use, speed, and excellent documentation. It is used for testing the functions as well as the components, with help from testing library.

- **Vue Testing Library:** A library that provides a set of utilities for testing Vue.js components. Vue Testing Library focuses on testing the component's public API, rather than its implementation details. This makes your tests more resilient to changes in the component's code. It has a great focus on testing what the user is seeing.
- **Cypress:** A powerful end-to-end testing framework that allows you to write tests that simulate real user interactions with your application. Cypress provides a rich set of features for writing and debugging E2E tests.

Test Driven Development (TDD): Why Start with the Test?

Test-Driven Development (TDD) is a software development process where you write tests *before* you write the code that implements the functionality. Here's how it works:

1. **Write a Test:** Write a test that describes the desired behavior of the code.
2. **Run the Test (It Should Fail):** Run the test. It should fail because you haven't written the code yet.
3. **Write the Code:** Write the minimum amount of code necessary to make the test pass.
4. **Run the Test (It Should Pass):** Run the test again. It should now pass.
5. **Refactor:** Refactor your code to improve its design and readability. Make sure that all tests still pass after refactoring.
6. **Repeat:** Repeat steps 1-5 for the next piece of functionality.

Benefits of TDD:

- **Clear Requirements:** Forces you to think about the requirements of your code before you start writing it.
- **Testable Code:** Encourages you to write more modular and testable code.
- **Reduced Debugging Time:** Helps you catch bugs early in the development process, reducing debugging time.

Personal Insight: The Mindset Shift: Tests are Code, Too!

The biggest hurdle I had to overcome when learning about testing was the mindset shift of thinking of tests as "real" code. Tests aren't just a chore to be completed after the "real" work is done; they are an integral part of the development process.

Conclusion: Building a Foundation of Confidence

Testing is an essential part of building robust, maintainable, and scalable Vue.js applications. By understanding the benefits of testing, the different types of tests, and the available testing tools, you can create a testing strategy that provides you with the confidence you need to deliver high-quality software. Let's get into creating those tests.

11.2 Unit Testing with Jest and Vue Testing Library – Testing the Smallest Pieces: Validating the Building Blocks

As we've discussed, unit tests form the bedrock of a robust testing strategy. They are small, isolated tests that verify the behavior of individual functions, modules, or classes in your Vue.js application. Unit tests focus on verifying the code is working as expected without concerning all the other pieces around the system.

In this section, we'll explore how to write effective unit tests using two popular tools: Jest and Vue Testing Library. We'll cover the basics of setting up Jest, writing unit tests for pure JavaScript functions, and using Vue Testing Library to test Vue.js components at a unit level.

Why Unit Tests? Isolation, Speed, and Precision

- **Isolation:** Unit tests focus on individual units of code, allowing you to isolate and test specific functionality without the interference of other parts of the application.
- **Speed:** Unit tests are typically fast to run, allowing you to quickly iterate on your code and get immediate feedback.
- **Precision:** Unit tests allow you to pinpoint exactly where a bug exists, making it easier to fix.

Setting Up Jest: Preparing Your Testing Environment

If you don't already have Jest set up in your Vue.js project, you'll need to install the following packages:

```
npm install --save-dev jest @vue/test-utils
# OR
yarn add --dev jest @vue/test-utils
```

- **jest:** The core Jest testing framework.
- **@vue/test-utils:** Provides utilities for mounting and interacting with Vue.js components in your tests.

You'll also need to create a jest.config.js file in the root of your project to configure Jest:

```
// jest.config.js
module.exports = {
  moduleFileExtensions: ['js', 'vue'],
  transform: {
    '^.+\\.js$': 'babel-jest',
    '^.+\\.vue$': '@vue/vue3-jest'
  },
  testEnvironment: 'jsdom',
  testMatch: ['**/tests/**/*.spec.js']
};
```

Key Configs:

- **js, vue**: These are the extensions to look at when reading in the code files.
- **babel-jest**: Javascript conversion code.
- **@vue/vue3-jest**: For Vue 3, allows you to test Vue code files.
- **testEnvironment**: Sets up basic environment.
- **testMatch**: This allows Jest to know the location of the test files.

To run the tests, you can add a test script to your package.json file:

```
"scripts": {
  "test": "jest"
}
```

Then, run the tests using npm or yarn:

```
npm test
# OR
yarn test
```

Writing Unit Tests for Pure JavaScript Functions: Testing the Logic

Let's start with a simple example of a unit test for a pure JavaScript function. A pure function is a function that always returns the same output for the same input and has no side effects. This makes them easy to test.

```
      // src/utils.js
export function capitalize(str) {
  if (!str) {
    return '';
  }
  return str.charAt(0).toUpperCase() + str.slice(1);
}

      // tests/unit/utils.spec.js
import { capitalize } from '@/utils';

describe('capitalize', () => {
  it('should capitalize the first letter of a string', () =>
{
    expect(capitalize('hello')).toBe('Hello');
  });

  it('should return an empty string if the input is empty',
() => {
    expect(capitalize('')).toBe('');
  });
});
```

Explanation:

- **describe:** The describe function is used to group related tests together. It takes a string that describes the group of tests.
- **it:** The it function is used to define an individual test case. It takes a string that describes the test case and a function that contains the test logic.
- **expect:** The expect function is used to make assertions about the expected behavior of the code. It takes a value as an argument and returns an object with various matcher methods.
- **.toBe:** The toBe matcher method is used to assert that two values are equal.

Testing Vue.js Components with Vue Testing Library: Focusing on User Interactions

While Jest can be used to test the internal logic of Vue.js components, Vue Testing Library provides a more user-centric approach. It encourages you to test the component's public API and to simulate how a user would interact with the component. This leads to tests that are more resilient to changes in the component's implementation details.

A Simple Example: Testing a Counter Component

Let's revisit our counter component from the previous chapter and write a component test using Vue Testing Library:

```
      // src/components/Counter.vue
<template>
  <div>
    <p>Count: {{ count }}</p>
    <button @click="increment">Increment</button>
  </div>
</template>

<script>
import { ref } from 'vue';

export default {
  setup() {
    const count = ref(0);

    const increment = () => {
      count.value++;
    };

    return {
      count,
      increment
    };
  }
};
</script>
```

```
      // tests/unit/Counter.spec.js
import { render, screen, fireEvent } from '@vue/test-utils';
import Counter from '@/components/Counter.vue';

describe('Counter.vue', () => {
  it('increments count when button is clicked', async () => {
    render(Counter); // Renders the counter object into a
virtual DOM

    const button = screen.getByText('Increment'); // Get
"increment button".
```

```
    const countElement = screen.getByText('Count: 0'); //Get
count text

    await fireEvent.click(button);

    expect(countElement).toHaveTextContent('Count: 1');
//Check if content changes
  });
});
```

Explanation:

- **render(Counter):** Use the render method to render the Counter component. This creates a virtual DOM representation of the component that you can interact with in your test.
- **screen.getByText('Increment'):** Use the screen.getByText() method to find the button and the count element by their text content.
- **await fireEvent.click(button):** Use the fireEvent.click() method to simulate a click on the button. This triggers the increment method in the component.
- **expect(countElement).toHaveTextContent('Count: 1'):** Use the expect() method to assert that the count element's text content has been updated to "Count: 1".

Key Principles for Effective Unit Testing:

- **Write Tests First:** Consider using Test-Driven Development (TDD) to write tests *before* you write the code. This will help you design more testable and modular code.
- **Focus on Public API:** Test the component's public API (props, events, and slots) rather than its implementation details. This will make your tests more resilient to changes in the component's code.
- **Keep Tests Isolated:** Make sure your unit tests are isolated and don't depend on external resources or dependencies. Use mocks and stubs to simulate external dependencies.
- **Write Clear and Concise Tests:** Write tests that are easy to read, understand, and maintain. Use descriptive test names and clear assertions.

Personal Insight: Start Small, Build Confidence

The thought of writing tests can be daunting. Unit tests, however, provide a good base. This will let you build and build upon a reliable system.

Conclusion: The Foundation of Quality

Unit testing is essential for building robust, reliable, and maintainable Vue.js applications. While this is only one section of the larger testing chapter, the core concepts here help you gain confidence. In the next step, we will see how component testing works.

11.3 Component Testing – Ensuring Individual Components Work Together: Validating the Building Blocks

With the basic functions covered with Unit Testing, it's time to test that components are working together. Unit testing is a crucial foundation, but it only verifies that individual functions or methods are working as expected. Component tests take a broader view, focusing on verifying that the different parts of a component work together correctly. This ensures that a collection of functions and data are still working.

Component tests are essential for ensuring that your Vue.js components are behaving as expected, that their templates are rendering correctly, and that they are properly interacting with their props, events, and state.

What Component Tests Should Cover: A Comprehensive Checklist

When writing component tests, you should aim to cover the following aspects of your components:

- **Template Rendering:** Verify that the component's template is rendering correctly based on its props and state.
- **Prop Handling:** Ensure that the component is receiving and processing props correctly.
- **Event Emission:** Verify that the component is emitting the correct events when certain actions are performed.
- **State Management:** Ensure that the component's state is being updated correctly in response to user interactions or other events.
- **Lifecycle Hooks:** Verify that the component's lifecycle hooks are being called at the appropriate times and that they are performing the expected actions.

Testing Tools

The same tools that are used for Unit Testing will be used again for Component Testing! In particular,

1. Jest is a way to organize tests, and set the scene.
2. Vue Testing Library is a way to access elements.

A Simple Component Test Walkthrough

Let's look at a common component.

```
    // src/components/Greeting.vue
<template>
  <div>
    <h1>{{ greeting }}</h1>
    <button @click="changeGreeting">Change Greeting</button>
  </div>
</template>

<script>
import { ref } from 'vue';

export default {
  props: {
    initialGreeting: {
      type: String,
      default: 'Hello, world!'
    }
  },
  setup(props) {
    const greeting = ref(props.initialGreeting);

    const changeGreeting = () => {
      greeting.value = 'Goodbye, world!';
    };

    return {
      greeting,
      changeGreeting
    };
  }
};
</script>
```

Let's walk through the key steps to testing this component.

1. Import Utilities

```
import { render, screen, fireEvent } from '@vue/test-utils';
import Greeting from './Greeting.vue';
```

render: Used to load in the component and its template.
screen: Used to query elements.
fireEvent: Used to click buttons, and simulate inputs.

2. Add the test using the tool you created.

```
describe('Greeting.vue', () => {
  it('renders the greeting prop', () => {
    render(Greeting, {
      props: {
        initialGreeting: 'Hello, Jest!'
      }
    });

    expect(screen.getByText('Hello,
Jest!')).toBeInTheDocument();
  });

  it('updates the greeting when the button is clicked', async
() => {
    render(Greeting);

    const button = screen.getByText('Change Greeting');
    await fireEvent.click(button);

    expect(screen.getByText('Goodbye,
world!')).toBeInTheDocument();
  });
});
```

And that's it! Your first component test has been created! To recap, it does the following things:

1. Check what happens when a specific prop value was used.
2. Simulate the user by changing a button and checking if the screen updates as expected.

Code Coverage: Measuring Your Testing Efforts

Code coverage is a metric that measures the percentage of your codebase that is covered by tests. It provides a way to assess the thoroughness of your testing strategy and to identify areas of your code that are not being adequately tested.

Jest provides built-in support for code coverage. To enable code coverage, you can add the --coverage flag to your test command:

```
        "scripts": {
  "test": "jest --coverage"
}
```

When you run the tests with the --coverage flag, Jest will generate a coverage report that shows you the percentage of lines, branches, functions, and statements that are covered by your tests.

Personal Insight: Component Tests Can Guide Architecture

A positive effect of my component testing has been helping guide the structure of my codebase. This is done by thinking out what's going to be tested, and finding a design pattern that works well with these tests.

Conclusion: Building Confidence in Your Components

Component tests are crucial for verifying the behavior of individual components. By writing comprehensive component tests, you can ensure that your components are working correctly and that they are properly interacting with their props, events, and state. Great job on ensuring that system works, now comes the grand finale of End-to-End testing.

11.4 End-to-End Testing with Cypress – From User Action to Application Response: Verifying the System as a Whole

While unit tests and component tests focus on individual parts of your application, end-to-end (E2E) tests take a holistic view, simulating real user interactions with your application and verifying that the entire system is working correctly from the user's perspective. E2E is the final test to make sure that the user can do what they expect.

Think of E2E tests as a final quality assurance check before your application is released into the wild. They ensure that all the pieces of your application are working together seamlessly and that the user can accomplish their goals without encountering any errors or unexpected behavior. They are the last stand for your project.

The Importance of E2E Tests: Seeing the Forest for the Trees

E2E tests are crucial for:

- **Verifying System Integration:** Ensuring that all the different parts of your application are working together correctly.
- **Simulating Real User Scenarios:** Testing your application in a way that closely mimics how real users will interact with it.
- **Identifying Complex Bugs:** Catching bugs that are difficult to identify with unit tests or component tests, such as issues related to routing, data flow, or user interface interactions.
- **Building Confidence:** Providing a high level of confidence that your application is working correctly before it is released to users.

Cypress: The Modern Choice for End-to-End Testing

While there are various E2E testing frameworks available, Cypress has emerged as the leading choice for modern web applications. Cypress offers a number of advantages over traditional E2E testing frameworks:

- **Time Travel:** Allows you to step back in time and see exactly what happened during each step of your tests.
- **Real-Time Reloads:** Automatically reloads your tests whenever you make changes to your code.
- **Automatic Waiting:** Automatically waits for elements to become visible and interactive before interacting with them.
- **Spies, Stubs, and Clocks:** Provides built-in support for spies, stubs, and clocks, making it easier to test complex scenarios.
- **Debuggability:** Has amazing debugging! Easily show all the errors in your project.

Installing Cypress: Adding the E2E Powerhouse to Your Project

To install Cypress in your Vue.js project, run the following command:

```
    npm install cypress --save-dev
# OR
yarn add cypress --dev
```

This will download the Cypress library and add it to your project's node_modules directory.

Configuring Cypress: Setting Up the Playground

After installing Cypress, you'll need to configure it for your project. This typically involves the following steps:

1. **Add Cypress scripts to your package.json file:**

```
{
  "scripts": {
    "cy:open": "cypress open",
    "cy:run": "cypress run"
  }
}
```

    - cy:open: Opens the Cypress Test Runner in interactive mode.
    - cy:run: Runs the Cypress tests in headless mode (useful for CI/CD).
2. **Open Cypress:**

    Run the cy:open script to open the Cypress Test Runner:

```
npm run cy:open
# OR
yarn cy:open
```

    This will open the Cypress Test Runner in a new window.

3. **Configure Cypress Project:**

    Cypress will automatically detect your project and prompt you to configure it. Follow the on-screen instructions to set up your project.

    - **Choose Component Testing or E2E Testing:** Select "E2E Testing" to configure Cypress for end-to-end testing.
    - **Configure Your Project:** Cypress will automatically detect your project's dependencies and suggest a configuration. You can customize this configuration as needed.
4. **Create a Cypress Configuration File:**
    Cypress will create a cypress.config.js (or cypress.config.ts) file in

the root of your project. This file contains the configuration options for Cypress. You can customize these options to suit your needs.

```
const { defineConfig } = require('cypress')

export default defineConfig({
  e2e: {
    setupNodeEvents(on, config) {
      // implement node event listeners here
    },
  },
})
```

Writing Your First E2E Test: Simulating a User Journey

Let's create a simple example of an E2E test that verifies that a user can navigate to the about page:

First create a basic test file in Cypress's E2E test examples folder

```
describe('Navigation', () => {
  it('should navigate to the about page', () => {
    cy.visit('/') // Visit the home page
    cy.contains('About').click() // Click the link with the
text "About"
    cy.url().should('include', '/about') // Assert that the
URL includes /about
    cy.get('h1').should('contain', 'About') // Assert that
the about page title is displayed
  })
})
```

Now it's time to run that code, enter into the console npm run cy:open, after it loads, click the 'E2E Testing' option, then pick a browser of your choice, finally you will be taken to the component tester!

Personal Insight: End-to-End: A Final Peace of Mind

End-to-end tests have given me a final sense of peace of mind before releasing my Vue.js applications. They allow me to verify that the entire system is working correctly from the user's perspective, ensuring that the application is ready for prime time.

Conclusion: A Robust Testing Strategy for Success

Testing your Vue.js applications is an essential part of the software development process. By understanding the benefits of testing, the different types of tests, and the available testing tools, you can create a testing strategy that provides you with the confidence you need to deliver high-quality software.
To summarize:

- Unit tests makes sure the small pieces are well.
- Component tests makes sure all those small parts together make a working component.
- E2E tests confirm that the entire app and system are in working order.

Now, to put the cherry on top of your development and testing, let's see how to deploy everything!

Chapter 12: Deployment and Optimization – Taking Your Vue.js Application Live and Beyond

Congratulations! You've built a fantastic Vue.js application, tested it thoroughly, and are ready to share it with the world. The final step is to deploy your application to a production environment and optimize it for performance and search engine visibility. This chapter will walk you through the entire deployment and optimization process.

This chapter will cover all the things that you need to do to send your site live! To start off, these are the things covered:

- Building your application in production mode
- Taking advantage of all the deployment tools available
- Optimizing performance of the application and
- Improving SEO and access.

12.1 Building for Production – Preparing for the Real World: Transforming Your Development Code into a Lean, Mean, Serving Machine

You've poured your heart and soul into building your Vue.js application, crafting elegant components, and meticulously managing state. Now, it's time to prepare your creation for the real world, transforming it from a development environment into a lean, mean, serving machine that can handle the demands of production traffic. This process, known as building for production, involves a series of optimizations and transformations that minimize the size and maximize the performance of your application.

Think of building for production as tuning a race car for the big race. You strip away any unnecessary weight, optimize the engine for maximum power, and fine-tune the suspension for optimal handling. Similarly, building your Vue.js application for production involves removing unused code, minimizing file sizes, and optimizing your assets for delivery over the web.

The Goal: Optimized Performance, Minimized Size

The primary goal of building for production is to optimize your application for performance and to minimize its size. This will result in faster load times, a smoother user experience, and reduced bandwidth consumption.

Key Objectives:

- To create something that has good network usage and won't slow user computers.

The build process aims to take the code and components you created, and prepare it for a wider audience with varying internet speeds and devices.

The Transformation: What Happens During the Build Process

The build process typically involves the following steps:

1. **Tree Shaking: Eliminating Dead Code**
   One of the most important optimizations performed during the build process is *tree shaking*. Tree shaking involves analyzing your application's code and removing any unused functions, variables, or modules. This can significantly reduce the size of your application, especially if you're using large libraries or frameworks that contain a lot of code that you don't actually need.
2. **Minification: Reducing Code Size**
   Minification is the process of reducing the size of your code by removing whitespace, comments, and other unnecessary characters. It also involves shortening variable names and function names to further reduce the size of your code.

   Minification can significantly reduce the size of your JavaScript and CSS files, resulting in faster load times.

3. **Code Splitting: Loading Code on Demand**
   Code splitting is the process of splitting your application into smaller chunks that can be loaded on demand. This allows you to reduce the initial load time of your application by only loading the code that is needed for the current view. Other code can then be loaded lazily as the user navigates to different parts of the application.
4. **Asset Optimization: Compressing and Resizing Images**
   Images can often be a significant contributor to the overall size of your application. Optimizing images involves compressing them to reduce their file size without sacrificing quality. It also involves

resizing images to the appropriate dimensions for the target display size.

5. **Other Asset Transformations**
   There is also asset bundling, where all the source files are combined into a few files for fast download.

Leveraging Vue CLI or Vite: The Recommended Path

The easiest and most effective way to build your Vue.js application for production is to use Vue CLI or Vite. These tools provide a streamlined build process that automatically performs all the necessary optimizations.

Building with Vue CLI:

To build your application for production using Vue CLI, simply run the following command in your project directory:

```
    npm run build
# OR
yarn build
```

This will create a dist directory in your project root, containing the production-ready build of your application. Vue CLI will automatically perform tree shaking, minification, code splitting, and asset optimization during the build process.

Building with Vite:

If you're using Vite, the command is the same:

```
    npm run build
# OR
yarn build
```

Vite's build process is even faster and more efficient than Vue CLI's, thanks to its use of esbuild and its ability to leverage native ES modules.

Understanding the Build Output: What's Inside the dist Directory

The dist directory (or whatever you configured as your output directory) will contain the following files:

- **index.html:** The main HTML file for your application.
- **js/:** A directory containing the JavaScript chunks for your application. These chunks are the result of code splitting and contain the minified and tree-shaken code for your components and modules.
- **css/:** A directory containing the CSS files for your application. These files are minified and may be split into multiple chunks for improved caching.
- **img/:** A directory containing the optimized images for your application. These images have been compressed and resized to reduce their file size.
- **favicon.ico:** The favicon for your application.

These are the only files that you need to deploy to your web server.

Inspecting the Build Output: Analyzing Your Application's Size

It's helpful to inspect the build output to understand the size of your application and to identify any areas that can be further optimized. Vue CLI and Vite provide tools for analyzing the build output and visualizing the size of your application's chunks. This process also helps discover issues that your application has, and resolve them before they are released to the public.

Production-Specific Configuration: Fine-Tuning Your Application for the Real World

In some cases, you may need to configure your application differently for production than for development. This can be done using environment variables or by creating separate configuration files for production and development.

Personal Insight: Building for Production: A Mark of Professionalism

Taking the time to properly build your Vue.js application for production is a sign of professionalism. It shows that you care about the user experience and that you're committed to delivering a high-quality product.

Conclusion: From Development to Deployment Readiness

Building your Vue.js application for production is an essential step in the deployment process. By understanding the optimizations that are performed during the build process and by using tools like Vue CLI or Vite, you can create a lean, mean, serving machine that is ready to handle the demands of production traffic. Let's move on to the deployment.

12.2 Deployment Options (Netlify, Vercel, AWS, Firebase) – Choosing the Right Home for Your Application: Finding the Perfect Hosting Solution

You've built your Vue.js application, optimized it for performance, and are now ready to share it with the world. But where do you host it? Choosing the right deployment option is crucial for ensuring that your application is reliable, scalable, and accessible to your users. There are many different options, each with its own strengths, weaknesses, and pricing models.

This section explores four popular deployment options for Vue.js applications: Netlify, Vercel, Amazon S3 with CloudFront, and Firebase Hosting. We'll delve into the features, benefits, and drawbacks of each option, helping you make an informed decision based on your specific needs and requirements.

Think of choosing a deployment option as finding the perfect home for your application. You need to consider factors like location, size, security, and cost to find the best fit for your needs.

The Landscape: A Comparison of Deployment Options

Feature	Netlify	Vercel	AWS S3 + CloudFront	Firebase Hosting
Ease of Use	Very Easy	Very Easy	Complex	Easy
Scalability	Excellent	Excellent	Excellent	Excellent
Cost	Competitive (Free Tier)	Competitive (Free Tier)	Pay-as-you-go	Competitive (Free Tier)
CDN	Built-in	Built-in	CloudFront	Built-in
SSL Certificates	Automatic	Automatic	Automatic	Automatic
Continuous Deployment	Built-in	Built-in	Requires configuration	Built-in
Serverless Functions	Built-in	Built-in	AWS Lambda	Cloud Functions for Firebase

Use Cases	Static Sites, SPAs	Static Sites, SPAs	Static Assets, Media	Static Sites, SPAs, Mobile Backends
Vendor Lock-in	Low	Low	High	Medium

Let's delve into each of these options to provide a complete guide.

Option 1: Netlify – The All-in-One Platform for Modern Web Projects

Netlify is a popular platform that streamlines the deployment and hosting of static websites and single-page applications. It's known for its ease of use, powerful features, and generous free tier.

Strengths of Netlify:

- **Simple and Intuitive:** Netlify provides a user-friendly interface and a simple deployment workflow that makes it easy to get your application live in minutes.
- **Continuous Deployment:** Netlify automatically builds and deploys your application whenever you push changes to your Git repository.
- **Automatic SSL Certificates:** Netlify automatically provisions and renews SSL certificates for your application, ensuring secure communication between your users and your server.
- **Global CDN:** Netlify uses a global content delivery network (CDN) to distribute your application's assets, reducing latency and improving performance for users around the world.
- **Serverless Functions:** Netlify supports serverless functions, allowing you to add dynamic functionality to your static website without managing a traditional server.
- **Form Handling:** Netlify provides built-in form handling capabilities, making it easy to collect data from your users.

Weaknesses of Netlify:

- **Limited Customization:** Netlify offers less customization than other deployment options, such as AWS S3 and CloudFront.
- **Vendor Lock-in:** While Netlify is relatively open, you are still tied to their platform and its features.

Deployment Process with Netlify:

1. **Sign Up for a Netlify Account:** Create a free Netlify account at https://www.netlify.com/.
2. **Connect Your Git Repository:** Connect your Git repository to Netlify. Netlify supports GitHub, GitLab, and Bitbucket.
3. **Configure Build Settings:** Specify the build command and the publish directory for your application. The build command should be npm run build or yarn build, and the publish directory should be dist.
4. **Deploy Your Application:** Netlify will automatically build and deploy your application.

Option 2: Vercel – The Platform for Frontend Developers

Vercel is another popular platform that focuses on providing a streamlined experience for frontend developers. It's known for its speed, simplicity, and excellent support for modern JavaScript frameworks.

Strengths of Vercel:

- **Fast Deployments:** Vercel is designed for speed, offering incredibly fast deployments and edge caching.
- **Automatic SSL Certificates:** Vercel automatically provisions and renews SSL certificates for your application.
- **Serverless Functions:** Vercel provides built-in support for serverless functions, allowing you to add dynamic functionality to your static website.
- **Preview Deployments:** Vercel automatically creates preview deployments for every pull request, allowing you to test changes before they are merged into the main branch.
- **GitHub Integration:** Vercel integrates seamlessly with GitHub, making it easy to deploy your application from your Git repository.

Weaknesses of Vercel:

- **Limited Customization:** Similar to Netlify, Vercel offers less customization than other deployment options.
- **Vendor Lock-in:** You are tied to their platform and its features.

Deployment Process with Vercel:

1. **Sign Up for a Vercel Account:** Create a free Vercel account at https://vercel.com/.

2. **Connect Your Git Repository:** Connect your Git repository to Vercel.
3. **Configure Build Settings:** Vercel will automatically detect your application's build settings. If necessary, you can customize these settings.
4. **Deploy Your Application:** Vercel will automatically build and deploy your application.

Option 3: Amazon S3 + CloudFront – Scalability and Control in the Cloud

Amazon S3 (Simple Storage Service) is a cloud storage service that allows you to store and serve static assets, such as HTML, CSS, JavaScript, and images. Amazon CloudFront is a content delivery network (CDN) that distributes your assets globally, reducing latency and improving performance for users around the world.

This combination provides a highly scalable and customizable solution for hosting your Vue.js application, but it also requires more technical expertise to set up and manage.

Strengths of Amazon S3 + CloudFront:

- **Scalability:** Amazon S3 and CloudFront are designed to handle massive amounts of traffic and data, making them ideal for applications with high scalability requirements.
- **Global Reach:** CloudFront has a global network of edge locations, ensuring that your assets are delivered quickly and efficiently to users around the world.
- **Customization:** Amazon S3 and CloudFront offer a high degree of customization, allowing you to fine-tune your hosting configuration to meet your specific needs.
- **Cost-Effective:** The pay-as-you-go pricing model can be very cost-effective for applications with variable traffic patterns.

Weaknesses of Amazon S3 + CloudFront:

- **Complexity:** Setting up and managing Amazon S3 and CloudFront can be complex, requiring technical expertise in cloud infrastructure.
- **Security:** Properly configuring security settings is crucial to prevent unauthorized access to your data.

- **Manual Deployment:** Deploying updates requires manually uploading files to S3 and invalidating the CloudFront cache.

Deployment Process with Amazon S3 + CloudFront:

1. **Create an S3 Bucket:** Create an S3 bucket to store your application's static assets.
2. **Upload Your Assets:** Upload the files from your dist directory to the S3 bucket.
3. **Create a CloudFront Distribution:** Create a CloudFront distribution to distribute your assets globally.
4. **Configure CloudFront to Use Your S3 Bucket:** Configure CloudFront to use your S3 bucket as the origin for your assets.
5. **Set Up DNS:** Point your domain name to the CloudFront distribution.

Option 4: Firebase Hosting – Google's Simplified Hosting Solution

Firebase Hosting provides a simpler and more cost-effective alternative to AWS S3 and CloudFront, while still offering a robust and scalable hosting solution. Firebase Hosting is particularly well-suited for applications that are already using other Firebase services, such as Firebase Authentication or Firestore.

Strengths of Firebase Hosting:

- **Easy to Use:** Firebase Hosting provides a simple and intuitive command-line interface (CLI) for deploying your application.
- **Automatic SSL Certificates:** Firebase Hosting automatically provisions and renews SSL certificates for your application.
- **Global CDN:** Firebase Hosting uses a global CDN to distribute your assets, reducing latency and improving performance.
- **Free Tier:** Firebase Hosting offers a generous free tier that is sufficient for many small to medium-sized applications.
- **Integration with Other Firebase Services:** Firebase Hosting integrates seamlessly with other Firebase services, such as Firebase Authentication, Firestore, and Cloud Functions.

Weaknesses of Firebase Hosting:

- **Vendor Lock-in:** You are tied to Google and Firebase.

- **Limited Customization:** Offers less customization than other deployment options.

Deployment Process with Firebase Hosting:

1. **Create a Firebase Project:** Create a new Firebase project in the Firebase console.
2. **Install the Firebase CLI:** Install the Firebase CLI globally using npm or yarn: npm install -g firebase-tools
3. **Initialize Firebase Hosting:** Initialize Firebase Hosting in your project directory using the Firebase CLI: firebase init hosting
4. **Configure Firebase Hosting:** Configure Firebase Hosting to use your dist directory as the public directory.
5. **Deploy Your Application:** Deploy your application to Firebase Hosting using the Firebase CLI: firebase deploy --only hosting

Personal Insight: The Importance of Automation

I've learned that automating the deployment process is essential for building a scalable and reliable application. By using tools like Netlify, Vercel, or Firebase Hosting, you can automate the build, deployment, and hosting of your application, freeing you from the tedious and error-prone task of manually managing your infrastructure.

Conclusion: Choosing the Right Home

Choosing the right deployment option for your Vue.js application depends on your specific needs and requirements. Consider factors like ease of use, scalability, cost, and the level of customization that you need. Each section will have positives and negatives, so weighing each aspect is important. Now the website is live, let's look into optimization to ensure that it's the best website possible!

12.3 Performance Optimization – Making Your Application Blazingly Fast: Delivering a Lightning-Fast User Experience

Deploying your Vue.js application is a significant achievement, but it's only the first step. To truly delight your users, you need to ensure that your application is blazingly fast. Performance optimization is the art of making your application load quickly, respond smoothly to user interactions, and consume minimal resources.

In the world of web development, performance is a key differentiator. Users are impatient and expect applications to load instantly. If your application is slow or unresponsive, you risk losing users and damaging your reputation.

This section explores the essential techniques for optimizing the performance of your Vue.js applications, covering everything from lazy loading and code splitting to image optimization and caching.

Think of performance optimization as tuning a race car for maximum speed. You need to fine-tune every aspect of the car, from the engine and suspension to the aerodynamics and tires, to squeeze out every last bit of performance.

The Core Principles: A Foundation for Optimization

Before diving into specific techniques, it's helpful to understand the core principles of performance optimization:

- **Minimize Request Size:** Reduce the size of the files that need to be downloaded by the browser. This includes HTML, CSS, JavaScript, images, and other assets.
- **Reduce the Number of Requests:** Minimize the number of HTTP requests that the browser needs to make to load the application. Each request adds latency, so it's important to reduce the number of requests as much as possible.
- **Optimize Rendering Performance:** Optimize the way your Vue.js components render to minimize the amount of work that the browser has to do.
- **Leverage Caching:** Use caching to store frequently accessed data and assets in the browser's cache or on a content delivery network (CDN).

Lazy Loading: Loading Components on Demand

Lazy loading is a technique that allows you to load components only when they are needed. This can significantly reduce the initial load time of your application by only loading the code that is required for the initial view.

Vue.js provides a built-in function called defineAsyncComponent that makes it easy to implement lazy loading:

```
    import { defineAsyncComponent } from 'vue';

const MyComponent = defineAsyncComponent(() =>
import('./MyComponent.vue'));
```

In this example, the MyComponent component will only be loaded when it is actually used in the template.

Benefits of Lazy Loading:

- **Reduced Initial Load Time:** Improves the initial load time of your application by only loading the code that is needed for the initial view.
- **Improved Performance:** Reduces the amount of JavaScript that the browser needs to parse and execute, improving the overall performance of your application.

Code Splitting: Breaking Down Large Bundles

Code splitting is the process of splitting your application into smaller chunks that can be loaded on demand. This allows you to reduce the size of the initial JavaScript bundle and to load code only when it's needed.

Modern build tools like Vue CLI and Vite automatically perform code splitting for you. They analyze your application's code and split it into chunks based on your application's routes, components, and modules.

Benefits of Code Splitting:

- **Reduced Initial Bundle Size:** Reduces the size of the initial JavaScript bundle, resulting in faster load times.
- **Improved Caching:** Allows the browser to cache different parts of your application separately, improving caching efficiency.

Tree Shaking: Eliminating Dead Code

Tree shaking is the process of removing unused code from your application. Modern JavaScript bundlers like Webpack and Rollup automatically perform tree shaking during the build process. They analyze your application's code and remove any functions, variables, or modules that are not actually used.

Benefits of Tree Shaking:

- **Reduced Bundle Size:** Reduces the size of your JavaScript bundles by removing unused code.
- **Improved Performance:** Reduces the amount of JavaScript that the browser needs to parse and execute, improving the overall performance of your application.

Image Optimization: Compressing and Resizing for the Web

Images are often a significant contributor to the overall size of your application. Optimizing images involves compressing them to reduce their file size without sacrificing quality. It also involves resizing images to the appropriate dimensions for the target display size.

There are several tools and techniques that you can use to optimize images:

- **Image Optimization Tools:** Use tools like TinyPNG, ImageOptim, or Compressor.io to compress your images.
- **Responsive Images:** Use the <picture> element or the srcset attribute on the <img> element to serve different image sizes based on the user's screen size.
- **Lazy Loading:** Use lazy loading to load images only when they are visible in the viewport.

Caching: Storing Data for Faster Access

Caching is a technique that involves storing frequently accessed data and assets in a cache so that they can be retrieved more quickly in the future. There are several types of caching that you can use in your Vue.js applications:

- **Browser Caching:** Use HTTP headers to instruct the browser to cache static assets, such as images, CSS, and JavaScript files.
- **Service Worker Caching:** Use a service worker to cache API responses and other dynamic data.
- **Server-Side Caching:** Use a server-side caching mechanism, such as Redis or Memcached, to cache frequently accessed data on the server.

Content Delivery Networks (CDNs): Distributing Your Assets Globally

Content delivery networks (CDNs) are a network of servers that are distributed around the world. CDNs are used to distribute your application's static assets, such as images, CSS, and JavaScript files, to users from the server that is closest to them. This reduces latency and improves the load time of your application.

Personal Insight: Perfomance is a core feature, not a setting!

I had a project where performance was an afterthought, and the impact really showed. This can be seen from how users don't continue to use a system, or how conversion drops on the e-commerce platform. I have a new philosophy, making performance part of the core design, which had big payoffs.

Conclusion: Aim for Zero Loading Time!

Performance optimization is an ongoing process. As your application evolves, you should continuously monitor its performance and make adjustments as needed to ensure that it provides a fast and responsive user experience. A big part of that is optimizing the project to rank high in searches.

12.4 SEO Considerations – Helping Search Engines Find Your Application: Making Your Content Discoverable

In today's crowded online landscape, it's not enough to just build a great Vue.js application; you also need to make sure that people can find it. Search engine optimization (SEO) is the process of optimizing your website to rank higher in search engine results pages (SERPs). A good SEO rank enables you to bring in more organic traffic.

While single-page applications (SPAs) traditionally presented challenges for SEO, modern techniques and tools have made it possible to create highly search-engine-friendly Vue.js applications.

This section explores the essential SEO considerations for Vue.js applications, providing practical guidance on how to make your content discoverable by search engines like Google, Bing, and DuckDuckGo.
The reason for SEO is not just website visits. If SEO is low, this can make it harder to test your applications through the website for E2E.

Think of SEO as building a well-marked trail through the forest. You need to make sure that search engines can easily find and follow the trail to discover the valuable content that your application has to offer.

The Challenge of SPAs: A Shifting Landscape

Traditional search engines relied on crawling HTML pages to understand the content of a website. However, SPAs present a challenge because they typically load a single HTML page and then use JavaScript to dynamically update the content. This means that the initial HTML page may not contain all of the content that the search engine needs to index the application properly.

Fortunately, modern search engines like Google have become much better at crawling and indexing JavaScript-based websites. However, there are still several steps you can take to ensure that your Vue.js application is search-engine-friendly.

Key SEO Strategies for Vue.js Applications

Here are the key components of an SEO-friendly Vue.js application:

1. **Server-Side Rendering (SSR): Delivering Fully Rendered HTML**

   Server-side rendering (SSR) involves rendering your Vue.js application on the server and sending the fully rendered HTML to the browser. This makes it easier for search engines to crawl and index your content, as they don't have to execute JavaScript to see the content.

   There are several frameworks and tools that can help you implement SSR in your Vue.js applications:

   - **Nuxt.js:** A popular Vue.js framework that provides a simple and intuitive way to build SSR applications.
   - **Vitepress**: A tool made for Vue for helping create basic documentation websites for SEO.
   - **Vue CLI with vue-server-renderer:** You can also use Vue CLI with the vue-server-renderer package to implement SSR in your Vue.js applications.
2. **Meta Tags: Providing Context to Search Engines**

Meta tags are HTML tags that provide information about your application to search engines. They are placed in the <head> section of your HTML page.

The most important meta tags for SEO are:

- **<title>:** Specifies the title of the page. This is the text that is displayed in the search engine results page.
- **<meta name="description" content="...">:** Provides a brief description of the page's content. This is often used as the snippet of text that is displayed in the search engine results page.
- **<meta name="keywords" content="...">:** Specifies a list of keywords that are relevant to the page's content.

It's important to use relevant and descriptive meta tags on every page of your application.

3. **Sitemap: Guiding Search Engines Through Your Application**

   A sitemap is an XML file that lists all of the URLs in your application. It helps search engines discover and index your content more efficiently.

   You can generate a sitemap manually or use a tool to automatically generate it for you. Once you have a sitemap, you should submit it to Google Search Console and Bing Webmaster Tools.

4. **Robots.txt: Controlling Search Engine Access**

   The robots.txt file is a text file that tells search engines which parts of your application they should not crawl. This is useful for preventing search engines from crawling pages that are not intended for public access, such as admin pages or private user profiles.

   You should create a robots.txt file in the root directory of your application and specify the pages or directories that you want to disallow.

Best Practices: A Checklist for SEO Success

Here's a checklist of best practices to follow when optimizing your Vue.js applications for SEO:

- Implement server-side rendering (SSR) using Nuxt.js or Vue CLI with vue-server-renderer.
- Use descriptive and relevant meta tags on every page.
- Create a sitemap and submit it to Google Search Console and Bing Webmaster Tools.
- Create a robots.txt file to control search engine access.
- Use descriptive and keyword-rich URLs.
- Provide alt text for all images.
- Use semantic HTML elements (e.g., <article>, <nav>, <aside>).
- Make sure your application is mobile-friendly.
- Ensure that your application is accessible to users with disabilities.

Personal Insight: SEO: A Continuous Process of Refinement

SEO is not a one-time task; it's an ongoing process of refinement. You should continuously monitor your application's search engine rankings and make adjustments to your SEO strategy as needed. A huge factor in whether or not users can access your system.

Conclusion: Getting Your Application Discovered

SEO is an essential consideration for any Vue.js application that wants to reach a wide audience. By implementing the strategies and best practices outlined in this section, you can make your application more discoverable by search engines and attract more organic traffic.

Now we have talked about everything! Testing and optimization are things that should always be considered. Hope this helps you create the app of your dreams!

Appendices

Enhancing Your Vue.js Workflow

These appendices provide concise overviews and helpful tips for two indispensable tools in the Vue.js ecosystem: Vue CLI and Vue Devtools. These tools are essential for streamlining your development process, debugging issues, and gaining insights into your application's behavior.

Appendix A: Vue CLI – Scaffolding and Managing Your Projects

Vue CLI (Command Line Interface) is the standard toolchain for rapid Vue.js development. It provides a wealth of features for scaffolding new projects, managing dependencies, and building your application for production.

Think of Vue CLI as your project management console, giving you access to a wide range of commands and utilities that simplify common development tasks. With this set up, you will have to manually set up the project yourself. This makes project startup easier.

Creating a New Project with Vue CLI: A Streamlined Start

One of the most common uses for Vue CLI is to create new Vue.js projects. To create a new project, run the following command:

```
vue create my-project
```

This will prompt you to choose a preset. You can choose a default preset or manually select features such as TypeScript, a CSS pre-processor, and testing tools.

Key Vue CLI Commands: Your Project Management Arsenal

Vue CLI provides a number of useful commands for managing your project:

- **vue serve:** Starts a development server that automatically reloads your application whenever you make changes to your code. This is the command you'll use most often during development.

- **vue build:** Builds your application for production. This command performs optimizations such as tree shaking, minification, and code splitting to reduce the size and improve the performance of your application.
- **vue inspect:** Inspects the Webpack configuration that Vue CLI uses to build your application. This is useful for debugging build issues or for customizing the build process.
- **vue add <plugin>:** Adds a plugin to your project. Plugins provide additional functionality, such as support for TypeScript, Vuex, or Vue Router.

Personal Insight: The CLI: The Fastest Start

I was really impressed by how quickly you can spin up a fully functional Vue.js project with Vue CLI. It allows you to focus on writing code rather than spending time configuring build tools and setting up project dependencies.

Appendix B: Vue Devtools – Debugging and Inspecting Your Components

The Vue Devtools is a browser extension that allows you to inspect your Vue.js components, track state changes, and debug performance issues. It's an indispensable tool for any Vue.js developer.

Think of Vue Devtools as a magnifying glass that allows you to see inside your Vue.js components and understand how they are working. It provides a wealth of information about your components, including their props, data, computed properties, and events.

Installation: Adding the Power of Inspection

The Vue Devtools extension is available for Chrome, Firefox, and Edge. You can install it from the Chrome Web Store, the Firefox Add-ons Marketplace, or the Edge Add-ons Store.

- Chrome: https://chrome.google.com/webstore/detail/vuejs-devtools/nhdogjmejiglipccpnnnanhbledajbnh
- Firefox: https://addons.mozilla.org/en-US/firefox/addon/vue-js-devtools/

Using Vue Devtools: A Tour of the Features

Once you've installed Vue Devtools, you can open it by right-clicking on any Vue.js application in your browser and selecting "Inspect" and click the Vue tab.

The Vue Devtools provides several panels:

- **Components:** This panel allows you to inspect the component tree and to view the props, data, computed properties, and events for each component.
- **Timeline:** This panel allows you to record and analyze the performance of your application. You can use the Timeline panel to identify bottlenecks and optimize your code for performance.
- **Vuex (If Applicable):** If your application uses Vuex, this panel allows you to inspect your application's state, mutations, and actions.
- **Routing:** This panel allows you to debug what the current value is of the route.

Personal Insight: Devtools is a Power-Up Tool

When a student tells me "this doesn't work" but won't show me the code, I know how much it would be helped by devtools!

Conclusion: Empowering Your Development Workflow

Vue CLI and Vue Devtools are essential tools for any Vue.js developer. By mastering these tools, you can streamline your development process, debug issues more effectively, and gain insights into your application's behavior. These are great skills to use in any Vue project.